RED SOX
ESSENTIAL

Everything You Need to Know to Be a Real Fan!

Jim Prime

TRIUMPH
B O O K S
CHICAGO

Library of Congress Cataloging-in-Publication Data

Prime, Jim.
    Red Sox essential : everything you need to know to be a real fan / Jim Prime.
        p. cm.
    ISBN-13: 978-1-57243-818-7
    ISBN-10: 1-57243-818-5
        1. Boston Red Sox (Baseball team)—Miscellanea.

GV875.B62P75 2006
797.357'640974461—dc22

                                                                    2005056883

This book is available in quantity at special discounts for your group or organization. For further information, contact:

Triumph Books
542 South Dearborn Street
Suite 750
Chicago, Illinois 60605
(312) 939-3330
Fax (312) 663-3557

Printed in U.S.A.
ISBN-13: 978-1-57243-818-7
ISBN-10: 1-57243-818-5
Design by Patricia Frey
Editorial production by Prologue Publishing Services, Oak Park, Illinois
All photos courtesy of AP/Wide World Photos
Portions of the chapter "Bill 'Spaceman' Lee: Rebel Without a Pause" are excerpted from Jim Prime's biography of Bill Lee, which appears in the book '75: The Red Sox Team That Saved Baseball (Cambridge, MA: Rounder Books, 2005).

To Glenna, Catherine, Jeffrey, and Sophie,
who, along with me,
constitute the Prime family.

Acknowledgments

Thanks to John DeCoste, Bill Nowlin, Bill Wilder, Karen Wilder, Bill Lee, and Glenna Prime.

A special thank you to the late Ed Walton, baseball historian and author of several books on the Boston Red Sox. Ed was always encouraging and helpful when this then-youthful writer was getting started.

Introduction

"Whoever wants to know the heart and mind of America had better learn baseball." American historian Jacques Barzun made this astute comment in 1954, and he could well have added: "And whoever wants to know the heart and mind of baseball had better learn about the Boston Red Sox."

If the Boston Red Sox didn't exist, someone would have had to invent them. Their bizarre and unlikely history reads like a novel coauthored by Stephen King and J. K. Rowling, with illustrations by Gahan Wilson and Charles M. Shulz. They are every fan's baseball nightmare; they are everyone's baseball fantasy. On a shady street in Everytown, U.S.A., populated by accountants, dentists, and Republican spin-doctors, they are the cool house on the corner where all the kids like to hang out.

The Boston Red Sox are America's Baseball Team. They are a microcosm of America, and when they play in ballparks across this land, they often seem to draw as many fans as the home team does. They represent the underdog in all of us and reflect our desire to better ourselves. They have "pulled themselves up by their bootstraps," "gone from rags to riches," and "lived the American Dream." They are Charlie Brown, Wile E. Coyote, and Scratchy all rolled into one. They are famous underachievers who finally got it right and kicked the football without Lucy yanking it away, caught and devoured that annoying Road Runner, and kicked the crap out of Itchy.

This is your essential Red Sox book, and the essence of the Boston Red Sox does not lie in dry statistics or facts. Mind you there are a wealth of statistics and facts included herein, but it is not a definitive book on Red Sox history by any means—nor is it meant to be. There are other books out there that provide that. The essence of the Boston Red Sox lies in the colorful, heroic, and sometimes downright goofy players who have worn the uniform over the past 104 years or so. They represent all eras and ethnicities. They have their own eccentricities. This book strives to capture the spirit of the Red Sox and what being a Red Sox fan is all about.

If you live in New England, this book is essential to your self-preservation; if you live in the United States, it will make you a better American; if you live in Turkistan, it will make you want to move to Boston and buy season tickets.

If you just moved to Boston or are contemplating such a move and want to succeed at your profession—if you wish to be accepted into New England society—this book is a must. Water cooler chatter about the Red Sox is inevitable, and your level of Red Sox knowledge can make or break your career. Even for diehards, Red Sox conversations can be mine-fields; if you make a misstep, you might as well have made a pass at the CEO's wife at the Christmas party. Imagine an informal conversation with your employer in which you casually refer to the Green Monster as being "*about* 30 feet high." There goes your promotion. Or you refer to Grady Little as a "great manager of pitchers." You'd better be prepared to duck the stapler being heaved at your head. Perhaps you go to Fenway, sit in the bleachers, and casually comment on what a fine fielder Manny Ramirez is. You may not make it out alive. Or maybe your minister or rabbi mentions Bill Buckner and you say something like: "Boy, he was a great defensive player, wasn't he?" There goes your chance for Eternal Life. Or, God forbid, you hear someone mention Babe Ruth's pitching exploits and you blurt out, "Babe Ruth pitched, too?" They have executed people in Salem for much less.

Let's assume that you are a native New Englander, steeped in the lore and legend of the Red Sox. Wouldn't it still be great to have all the facts at hand in an easy-to-access format? When rich Uncle Theodore (named after the Splendid Splinter, of course) from Marblehead asks you at Christmas dinner if his namesake ever hit an inside-the-park homer, you'll be able to answer immediately, thereby ensuring your place in the will. Or when obnoxious Cousin Mickey from Connecticut, that border state that harbors an indeterminate number of Yankees sympathizers, claims that Joe was better than Ted, or Munson was tougher than Fisk, you will be well-armed with enough anecdotal ammo to wipe smug from his mug.

When a coworker casually comments that Kevin Millar must surely be the worst first baseman the Red Sox ever had, you can look at him tolerantly and say with great certainty: "Not even close," explaining that this honor goes to Dick "Dr. Strangeglove" Stuart, who was so bad he once got a standing ovation for successfully scooping up a candy bar wrapper that had blown onto the field. Your street cred will be instantaneously established.

This book will enable you to call any one of the Boston sports talk shows and go toe-to-toe with the loudest and most obnoxious hosts that the airwaves have to offer. In fact, you may actually be able to out-anecdote and out-obnoxious them, even if you can't out-analyze them.

The Boston Red Sox are one of baseball's oldest and most revered franchises. Their history all but encompasses the history of the professional game and in many ways reflects the 20th-century history of America. The franchise was progressive enough to install electric lights in 1947, and at the same time regressive enough to be the last to see the light and integrate.

Everything you should know about the Bosox is included herein: the heroes, the villains, the thrill of victory, and the agony of defeat. We explore the greatest hitters in Red Sox history, who just happen to be among the greatest hitters in baseball history. We delve into the greatest pitchers in Boston history, who just happen to be among the greatest pitchers in baseball history. Just for fun, we will also rank the greatest characters in Red Sox history, and they are an organization rich in memorable flakes.

We also provide the fan with a handy reference for milestones in Red Sox history. We rank the greatest moments and the biggest disappointments, the biggest goats and the biggest heroes.

We also explore the personalities that make the Red Sox such an endearing and captivating team: the exodus of Babe Ruth, the dramatic exit of Ted Williams, the tragedy of Tony Conigliaro, the comic opera of Bill Lee and Mickey McDermott—they are all here.

We dabble in trivia—and no team is better suited to trivia than the Sox. We also enter the realm of fantasy with some compelling "If Only..." scenarios that will jumpstart your imagination.

And we give you the numbers. Any baseball fan knows that the numbers 60'6" and 90' represent the respective distances between the mound and home plate, and between the bases. To be a true Red Sox fan, you must immediately and automatically know the significance of certain other numbers. As soon as someone mentions No. 9, you must know that they are referring to Ted Williams. Same with Yastrzemski's No. 8. You must know that, along with those famous digits, Nos. 1, 4, and 27 are the uniform numbers of Bobby Doerr, Joe Cronin, and Carlton Fisk, and that these numbers can be seen on the right field roof façade at Fenway Park. They have all been retired.

You must know that 310' indicates the distance from home plate to the left-field wall (though it may be somewhat less than accurate). You should also be aware that 302' represents the distance down the right field line. You must know the number 502, because that is the number of feet Ted Williams hit a home run into the right field bleachers on June 9, 1946. You must know that Manny Ramirez hit one over the light stanchion behind the Green Monster on June 23, 2001, that officially—and suspiciously—was estimated at 501'. (You don't mess with the legend of Teddy Ballgame, mister.)

Throughout this book, we will test you with significant—and totally insignificant—numbers. This is not a math test, but it will make you a more knowledgeable fan.

If you are ever captured by federal agents, charged with spying for, say, the Evil Empire, and interrogated by John Henry and Larry Lucchino under the bright lights of the Citgo sign to prove that you are, indeed, a member of Red Sox Nation, here are some inside stories that will help to prove your loyalty. This is your passport.

Cy, Babe, and Other Icons, 1901–1919

For 86 years the Boston Red Sox had been the punch line for more bad jokes than the Clinton presidency, both Bush administrations, and that collective entity known as "mothers-in-law" put together. For 86 years they were the laughingstock of baseball, a subject of ridicule, even to their own fans. After the California Angels won the World Series in 2002, David Letterman cracked that "It took the Angels 42 years to win a World Series—or as the Boston Red Sox call it, 'beginner's luck.'" Now that the Red Sox have finally won the World Series and are perennial contenders for American League honors, things will no doubt change. Already celebrity sightings at Fenway are starting to intrude on TV broadcasts, and the queue for jumping off the Sagamore Bridge has dwindled to practically nothing. Yes, things are quite different in Red Sox Nation now that the Sox have broken the "Curse of the Bambino."

When people think of the early days of the Boston Red Sox, they usually think of the disastrous sale of Babe Ruth to the Yankees in 1920, establishing the curse that would become an agonizing 86-year World Series drought. They think of two eras: the Ruth Red Sox and the Ruthless Red Sox. In actual fact, before Ruth made his first appearance in a Boston uniform in 1914, the franchise had already been in existence for 13 years and had won three pennants and two World Series.

The Boston Red Sox were one of the original franchises of the American League when it officially became baseball's second major league in the fall of 1900. Originally made up of players coaxed or stolen from the more established National League, the American League was soon on an even playing field with its elder sibling.

TRIVIA

Who got the first hit for Boston's American League franchise?

Answers to the trivia questions are on pages 175–176.

The first Boston clubs were known variously as the Americans, Puritans, Plymouth Rocks, and Somersets. (Pilgrims was briefly a nickname for the team, but was never an official team name.) The 1901 team finished second to the Chicago ballclub, with a 79–57 record, and Buck Freeman emerged as the first bona fide Boston star, leading the team in average (.339), homers (12), and RBIs (114). The next year they fell to third, followed by two first-place finishes. Early Red Sox stars included Freeman, Cy Young, and Jimmy Collins. Young and Collins led the Bostonians to the American League pennant in 1903, earning them the right to participate in the first ever "world series" of baseball against the National League champion Pittsburgh Pirates. Boston won that first World Series—a best-of-nine affair—five games to three. In 1904 they also captured the AL pennant, but the NL champion New York Giants refused to play them.

When you win the first World Series, you have no place to go but down, and for several years the Boston franchise did just that. In fact, they dropped all the way to the bottom of the league before rebounding in 1912 in a brand new ballpark called Fenway. That year they won the pennant and then toppled the New York Giants in the World Series. Now officially known as the Red Sox (owner John I. Taylor dubbed them the Red Sox in 1907, apparently without any ironic ideas about the connection between Sox and "defeat"), they boasted the best pitching in baseball, led by a fireballer called Smoky Joe Wood and a hot-hitting center fielder with unmatched range in Tris Speaker.

TRIVIA

Who did Boston play in their very first game as an American League franchise? And what was the score?

Answers to the trivia questions are on pages 175–176.

By the time Babe Ruth arrived to bolster the pitching staff, the Red Sox were already a powerhouse. With the Babe, they won their fourth pennant in 1915 and captured yet another World Series, this time besting the NL's Philadelphia Phillies. Even when Smoky Joe ruined his shoulder, Babe stepped

THE BOSTON RED SOX 1918
LAWLER MILLER JONES THOMAS RUTH HOOPER MAYS SHEAN KINNEY STRUNK M°INNIS BARROW
SCOTT DUBUC BUSH WHITEMAN SCHANG MAYER WAGNER AGNEW COFFEY
MASCOT & BATBOY

The 1918 Boston Red Sox beat the Chicago Cubs 4–2 to win the World Series. No team scored more than three runs in any game, and no home runs were hit. It would be 86 years before the Red Sox were champions again.

up and won 23 games to lead the Sox to the 1916 pennant—their fifth—and another World Series win over Brooklyn.

In December 1916 the Red Sox were sold to Broadway entrepreneur Harry Frazee, a watershed—many would say disastrous—event in club history. Frazee was a part-time owner, and his true love was Broadway, not Fenway. In an effort to cut the payroll—and as part of a league-wide salary reduction campaign (early collusion?)—he started to unload players such as Tris Speaker. The Sox finished second in 1917, but rallied in 1918 to take the pennant and then beat the Chicago Cubs for their fifth World Series championship. The Boston Red

TRIVIA

What pitcher won the first home game in Red Sox history?

Answers to the trivia questions are on pages 175–176.

3

TRIVIA

What was the brand-new home field of the fledgling Boston franchise?

Answers to the trivia questions are on pages 175–176.

Sox were the best team in baseball yet again, and it looked like a dynasty in the making.

Frazee put a quick end to those dreams by trading 15 players within five years, mostly to the Yankees, who became an instant powerhouse. Household names like Harry Hooper, Speaker, Ruth, Herb Pennock, Waite Hoyt, and Red Ruffing all disappeared from Boston.

Frazee's actions represented not so much a passing of the torch as a torching of the past.

By the NUMBERS

86—This number holds obvious significance, as the number of years between world championships in 1918 and 2004.

.406—Signifies the last player to bat .400 in the majors: Ted Williams in 1941. 521 and .344, two other must-know numbers, represent Ted's career home-run total and lifetime batting average.

1918, 1946, 1967, 1975, 1978, 1986, 2003, and 2004—All significant numbers for Red Sox fans: the first and last represent jubilation, the middle six varying degrees of frustration.

Denton True "Cy" Young: Pitching Personified

When they name baseball's most prestigious pitching award after you, chances are you were a pretty good hurler. Cy Young won 511 games in the major leagues. To put that number in perspective, that's only 17 less than Sandy Koufax and Warren Spahn *combined,* and Spahn has more victories (363) than any southpaw in history. In fact, Young's 316 losses are also more than any pitcher in history, despite a win-loss percentage of .618. As you might expect, any player named after a cyclone was not a finesse pitcher. Cy's bread and butter was the fastball, with which he fanned 2,803 batters in his 22-year career. While with the Red Sox, he led the American League in wins in three consecutive seasons (1901–1903), and in two of those years won more than 30 games!

What Babe Ruth later became to batting, Cy Young was to pitching. The Red Sox were fortunate to have had the services of both.

When Cy Young was 89 years old, a young reporter asked him politely if he'd ever pitched in the major leagues. Young replied, "Son, I won more games than you'll ever see." Assuming the reporter went on to report on fewer than 511 games in his unfolding career, the claim was no exaggeration.

Young arrived in the majors fresh from the farm—no, not the farm *team,* from an actual farm in Ohio. His arms dangled far beyond the sleeve of a suit that was several sizes too small for his 6'2", 210-pound frame. He was carrying a cardboard suitcase. Chicago's Cap Anson, a veteran ballplayer, thought that Young was a country bumpkin and greeted him as "Rube." The fireballing rookie responded to the ridicule with a three-hitter, and it was quickly decided that "Cyclone"—shortened to "Cy"—would be a much more appropriate nickname, since it was also the woeful sound coming from hitters on their way back to the dugout after striking out.

Cy Young won 511 games in his 22-year career. He joined the Red Sox in 1901, their charter year, and won 179 games, including two seasons with more than 30 wins and four others with more than 20 wins.

Red Sox Cy Young Award Winners

Name	Year	Record	ERA
Jim Lonborg	1967	22–9	3.16
Roger Clemens	1986	24–4	2.48
Roger Clemens	1987	20–9	2.97
Roger Clemens	1991	18–10	2.62
Pedro Martinez	1999	23–4	2.07
Pedro Martinez	2000	18–6	1.74

By the NUMBERS

33—Cy Young's age when he joined the Boston team.

33, 32, 28—The numbers of wins he racked up in his first three years in Boston.

83—The number of minutes it took Cy Young to pitch a perfect game in 1904.

27—The number of batters faced by Young when he pitched a no-hitter against New York on June 30, 1908. It was his third no-hit game.

The Ruthian Red Sox

Babe Ruth may be the personification, the embodiment, if not the trademark, of the New York Yankees, but it was as a member of the Boston Red Sox that the Bambino first attracted national attention. In those days he was tall, athletic, and minus the familiar beer belly that we associate him with today. In fact, he was almost lithe. He was also a pitcher.

Ruth joined the Red Sox in 1914 fresh from Baltimore of the Eastern League. Over the next six seasons, Ruth won a total of 89 games for the Sox. He had consecutive seasons of 18, 23, and 24 wins, leading the league with an incredible 35 complete games in 1917. In 1916 he boasted a league-best ERA of 1.75 and recorded nine shutouts, also tops in the American League.

In 1918 Ruth's pitching record was 13–7 and his ERA was still microscopic at 2.22, but he also led the league in homers with 11. The following year, 1919, the Red Sox dropped to sixth place as Frazee began to unload players to the New York Yankees. At his request, the Red Sox were now playing Ruth in the outfield, and the Babe responded to everyday position play by slugging the unprecedented total of 29 home runs. (The previous Red Sox high was 13 by Buck Freeman in 1903. Freeman had become the Red Sox first home run champion with 12 in 1901). Such gaudy numbers were unheard of and actually represented over 10 percent of the homers hit in the entire eight-team American League that year. He out-homered four entire teams, and the rest of his Red Sox teammates added only four more homers to the team total. Baseball saw the excitement generated by the home run, and the very next season decided to liven up the ball.

IF ONLY . . . Pedro Martinez had pitched to Babe Ruth. Pedro once challenged reporters to dig up the Babe so he could "drill him in the ass." But that was a visceral and understandable reaction to the non-stop talk of the Curse of the Bambino. In actual fact, it would have been an interesting match-up. Ruth was an intelligent hitter; Pedro is an intelligent pitcher. Pedro likes to intimidate. Ruth had the advantage of being able to think like a pitcher as well as a hitter. Ruth would have taken him deep the first time up and struck out swinging the second. There would be no brush-back pitch. Too much respect. Besides, if Pedro went back in time, he would have had to bat, too. Who knows, maybe Babe would have turned the tables and pitched to *him*. And drilled *him* in the ass.

Notwithstanding these achievements, in the winter following this breakout season, Frazee sold Babe Ruth to the New York Yankees for $100,000 and a mortgage of $300,000 on Fenway Park. It has been widely reported that he was strapped for cash, but baseball historians Glenn Stout and Richard Johnson have found convincing evidence to refute this claim. Frazee was scorned and vilified by press and public alike, and to this day when Red Sox fans meet at bars or online, his name is still mentioned in the same breath as Benedict Arnold and usually preceded with a colorful adjective or two.

Some Sox historians believe that the vilification of Harry Frazee was out of proportion to his actions and that such hatred may have been born of anti-Semitism—not only a case of religious intolerance but of downright ignorance, since Frazee was, in fact, a Presbyterian and a Mason, according to Stout. Whatever the case, Harry Frazee's name would be mud in New England for generations to come.

Long before Babe Ruth became baseball's greatest slugger, he was among the best left-handed pitchers in baseball. In 1916 he posted an ERA of 1.75; in 1917, it was 2.01. During the 1918 World Series, the last one the Red Sox would win for 86 years, Ruth was an integral cog in the winning machinery. The Boston manager of the day was Ed Barrow, and before Game 5 of the Series, he sat down with the Babe to go over the Chicago Cubs hitters. Barrow was especially adamant that Ruth be careful with Leslie Mann. "He's a plate-crowder," warned Barrow. "He'll force you

Babe Ruth helped lead the Red Sox to three World Series victories by winning five Series games as a pitcher before infamously being traded to the Yankees in 1920.

outside. Pitch under his chin to keep him back." Ruth listened intently and promised to follow his skipper's advice. And so he did. He threw the ball under the batter's chin and deposited him on his posterior. The hitter slowly got to his feet and dusted himself off, exchanging hostile looks with Ruth. Babe went into his wind-up and once again knocked the hitter down with some well-placed chin music. On the next pitch, the shaken batter was an easy out, and Ruth strode to the dugout to receive well-deserved accolades from his manger. "Well, Ed," he said, "I sure got that guy Mann away from the plate." Not bothering to look up, Barrow replied dryly, "Not yet, you haven't! Mann hasn't been at bat yet. You've been knocking down poor Max Flack." A clear case of taking some Flack for knocking down the wrong Mann.

By the NUMBERS

4–3—The final score in Babe Ruth's winning debut as a Red Sox pitcher on July 11, 1914. He defeated the Cleveland Naps.

26—The number of batters faced by Ernie Shore, June 23, 1917, in pitching an almost perfect game* in relief when Babe Ruth was ejected in the first inning for arguing a call. Shore had inherited a runner at first base, but he was erased trying to steal. Shore retired the next 26 batters.

*The Shore game is no longer considered a "perfect game" by MLB. The official definition of a perfect game says that a pitcher can permit no baserunners over a full nine innings (or extra innings) contest. Even though all 27 outs were made with Shore on the mound, the rule also states that the pitcher must pitch a complete game victory.

When Ruth came to the Red Sox in 1914 as a raw 19-year-old rookie, he roomed with fellow pitcher Ernie Shore. It wasn't long before Shore went to player-manager Bill Carrigan and demanded a new roommate. "I thought you were old friends," said a surprised Carrigan. "We are," said Shore. "But there's a place where friendship stops. A man wants some privacy in the bathroom. Just this morning I told him he was using my toothbrush, and he said, 'That's okay, I'm not particular!'"

Red Sox Manager Ed Barrow had been urged to move Ruth to the outfield in 1919, according to his former teammate and fellow Hall of Famer Harry Hooper. "Everett Scott, Heinie Wagner, and I went to Ed Barrow and suggested putting Babe in the outfield," Hooper once said. "'Nothing doing!' said Ed. 'Why, I would be the laughingstock of the league if I put the best left-handed pitcher in the league in the outfield.'" Hooper tried to reason with the stubborn skipper. "Barrow told us he had $50,000 invested in the club," recalled Hooper. "One day I said, 'Ed, you have big money in the club. You are interested in hearing the turnstiles click. Have you noticed we have a larger crowd when Ruth pitches?' 'Sure,' he answered. 'Ed,' I said, 'the crowds are coming out to see him hit. Why don't you put him in the outfield where he will be in the lineup every day?'" Hooper was finally successful in convincing Barrow that

TRIVIA

What was Duffy's Cliff?

Answers to the trivia questions are on pages 175–176.

TRIVIA

What was Babe Ruth's uniform number while he was with the Red Sox?

Answers to the trivia questions are on pages 175–176.

the scheme was worth a try, but added: "We'll put him in the outfield, but mark my words, the first big slump he gets in he will be back on his knees begging me to pitch." Hooper's biggest problem was that he played center field between Ruth and a left fielder named Roth. Both outfielders were wildly unpredictable, and Hooper soon decided for his own protection to move back to the safety of right field and let the Roth-Ruth combination fight it out for fly balls in left and center.

While still a member of the Boston Red Sox, Ruth (who used the heaviest bat in the league) hit a tremendous home run in a spring training contest in Florida. It exited the ballpark, soared over an adjacent racetrack, and landed in a farmer's pasture.

The assembled writers did some crude estimates and declared that the ball had traveled approximately 630 feet. Many observers disagreed, questioning the math credentials of the baseball reporters. New York writer Bill McGeehan defended their calculations. "All I know is, when it came down, it was covered in ice," claimed McGeehan.

Ruth's Red Sox teammate, fellow pitcher Joe Bush, once commented on Babe's large nose and upturned nostrils. "If he ever fell asleep out in the rain, he'd drown," he said.

Tris Speaker, a great fielder himself, once included Ruth in the top five or six defensive outfielders he'd seen.

Tris Speaker:
The Grey Eagle Soars

Tris Speaker was an outfielder with an infielder's instincts and quickness. The center fielder played shallow enough to act as an extra infielder, making unassisted double plays on shallow pop flies and was even involved in four 8–3 twin killings, something you are unlikely to see in today's game. In total he was involved in a record 139 double plays, and if the DP is the pitcher's best friend, Speaker must have been buddies with a lot of Red Sox throwers. His unique approach to outfield play enabled him to record 450 lifetime assists. Somehow he was still able to use his speed to go back on long drives and make the catches. With Harry Hooper and Duffy Lewis playing on either side of him, the opposing batters must have despaired of ever following Wee Willie Keeler's advice of "hitting them where they ain't."

While he revolutionized and redefined outfield play, the man known as Grey Eagle also wielded a powerful bat. He had a .345 lifetime average (one point higher than Ted Williams' .344) and batted .375 or better six times. Speaker's signature hit was the double, the money/glamour hit of the dead-ball era.

"Spoke," as his teammates called him, led the league in two-baggers eight times in his career, twice as a member of the Red Sox, and established the major league record with 792. He had a then-record (since surpassed) 53 in 1912 alone. In fact—like Yaz's 1967 and Ted's 1941—1912 was his signature season. He and his roommate Smoky Joe Wood (34-game winner) led the Red Sox to an incredible 105 victories and only 47 defeats during the regular season and spearheaded the World Series victory over the New York Giants. He had a 20-game hit streak from May 27 to June 15, and after a two-game drought, embarked on a 30-game streak. During the latter hit-a-thon

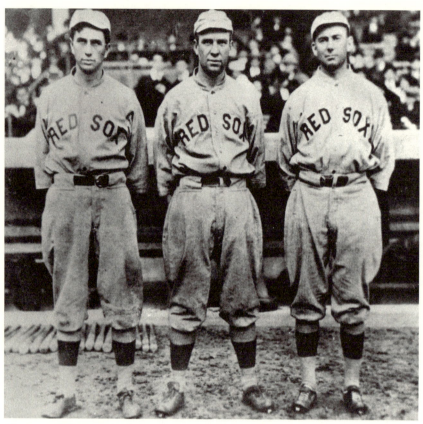

The core of the great Red Sox teams of the early 1910s was, from left, right fielder Harry Hooper, center fielder Tris Speaker, and left fielder Duffy Lewis.

the Red Sox won 23 of 30 games. On July 16 that streak came to a halt, but Speaker began another 20-game streak on July 24 of that year. There were also streaks of 13 and 12 games. From May 27 to August 14, a period of 80 days, he hit in 74 of 78 games and batted .424. In all, he hit safely in 130 games and plated a run in 96 of those games. His season batting average was .383, behind only Ty Cobb, who picked that year to bat .410, and "Shoeless" Joe Jackson (.395). He had a league best 53 doubles, 12 triples, and tied for the

TRIVIA

On April 20, 1912, Fenway Park first opened its doors. Front page news in Boston, surely? Nope. Why not?

Answers to the trivia questions are on pages 175–176.

By the NUMBERS

84—The record number of outfield assists recorded by Duffy Lewis, Tris Speaker, and Harry Hooper in 1913.

7–6—The score of the first official game at Fenway Park on April 20, 1912. The Red Sox defeated the New York Highlanders (who later became the New York Yankees) in eleven innings.

AL lead in homers with 10. He drew 82 bases on balls, tops for the Sox that year. Speaker also used his frequent visits to first, second, and third to steal 52 bases. Naturally, he won that year's MVP award, then known as the Chalmers Award.

Speaker's home-run total for 1912 had been recorded as nine, but about 60 years later writer Ed Walton discovered a "missing" homer, and the major league records committee made the change—pulling him even with "Home Run" Baker at 10.

"It would be useless for any player to attempt to explain successful batting," Speaker once concluded.

TRIVIA

Where did Fenway Park get its name?

Answers to the trivia questions are on pages 175–176.

Harry Hooper: Unknown Star

Hall of Famer Harry Hooper was one-third of one of the greatest outfield trios of all time, the so-called "million dollar outfield" (presumably, it would be "billion dollar outfield" in today's dollars). The other members were left fielder Duffy Lewis and center fielder Tris Speaker. They played together for six full seasons and led the Red Sox to World Series championships in 1912 and 1915. Hooper was the first player to slide on his backside in pursuit of a fly ball. "I like to recall that I was the inventor of the 'rump slide' in making a diving catch—to save teeth and elbows by sliding feet first instead of head first," he recalled in 1957.

Asked about his biggest thrill in baseball, Hooper chose the final game of the 1912 World Series against the New York Giants: "It was the eighth game, each team having won three, with one tie. In that game, in the ninth inning, I robbed Larry Doyle of a sure home run with a barehanded catch. It would have meant the ballgame. So it was that at the end of nine, we were tied 1–1. The Giants scored in the tenth and it was 2–1. Fred Snodgrass muffed Clyde Engel's easy fly. I bunted two pitches foul and then hit a drive. Snodgrass grabbed it where he had no business being. Steve Yerkes worked Christy Mathewson for a pass. Speaker hit a high foul. [Fred] Merkle went after it. Mathewson yelled to [Chief] Meyers, the catcher to make the catch. Meyers missed it. Speaker laughed and yelled to Mathewson: 'You called the wrong shot.' Speaker hit to right and the score was tied. Lewis was passed to get to Larry Gardner. Gardner hit a long fly, and we won the ballgame."

Hooper hit two home runs in the 1915 World Series, in the midst of the dead-ball era, and used his patented "rump slide" to catch a long fly from Casey Stengel and fire to double Zack Wheat off of third.

TOP TEN

Red Sox Regular-Season Stolen Base Leaders

	Name	Year	Stolen Bases
1.	Tommy Harper	1973	54
2.	Tris Speaker	1912	52
3.	Tris Speaker	1913	46
4.	Tris Speaker	1914	42†
	Otis Nixon	1994	42†
6.	Harry Hooper	1910	40†
	Bill Werber	1934	40†
8.	Harry Hooper	1911	38
9.	Harry Lord	1909	36
10.	Patsy Dougherty	1903	35†
	Tris Speaker	1909	35†
	Tris Speaker	1910	35†

Hooper batted left and threw right. He joined the Red Sox in 1909 and remained there until he was traded to the Chicago White Sox in 1921. On May 30, 1913, Hooper became the first player to homer leading off both games of a doubleheader. The feat stood for 80 years until Rickey Henderson matched it in 1993. Hooper played for four World Series champions, the Red Sox of 1912, 1915, 1916, and 1918.

In a letter from Harry Hooper to baseball historian Ellery Clark, dated April 8, 1974, Hooper explained how the famous outfield of Lewis-Speaker-Hooper came about:

"I played my first year, 1909, in left field. Started in right but couldn't handle the sun....But while I played left in 1909, I practiced playing the sun field until I was good at it....In 1910 Duffy Lewis came up....But Duffy couldn't play the sun field. So they shifted me to right and put Duffy in left, and from that day he never played any field except left. That was the beginning of the outfield Lewis-Speaker-Hooper." Duffy Lewis remembered that Red Sox managers would sometimes move Hooper from right to left against right-handed pull hitters.

TRIVIA

How many times has a Red Sox player captured the American League batting crown?

Answers to the trivia questions are on pages 175–176.

17

Notable but Overlooked Pitchers in Red Sox History

"Smoky" Joe Wood

Smoky Joe Wood is one of the most underrated players in baseball history. Those who saw him play described his talent with slack-jawed adoration. Walter "Big Train" Johnson, possessor of a blazing fastball, was once asked if he could throw faster than Wood. His answer: "Son, no one can throw a baseball faster than Joe Wood." Wood was with the Red Sox from 1908 to 1915, and who can say what he might have accomplished if not for an injury that curtailed his pitching career?

Smoky Joe had a Red Sox ERA of 1.99 while winning 117 games and losing only 56. In 1911 he spun a no-hitter against the St. Louis Browns. In 1912 he led the Boston AL franchise to the World Series title, winning a Red Sox record 34 games against only five losses. Many claim that this is the best pitching record of the century, and it would be difficult to refute the claim. He also had 258 strikeouts with an ERA of 1.91 that year. Once in the Series, he won three more games to clinch the title. Wood's last year in Boston was arguably his strongest. He went 15–5 and crafted a 1.49 ERA.

Dutch Leonard: An ERA for Any Era

Although the American League did not begin recording earned-run averages until 1913, statisticians have meticulously researched raw data from the preceding years to discover how pitchers performed in the earliest part of the 20th century. It turns out that Dutch Leonard of the Boston Red Sox established and still holds the record for lowest ERA for an entire major league season. The figure is astonishing: 0.96 earned runs per nine innings set in 1914. Opponents batted a less-than-lusty .180 against him,

By the NUMBERS

47,627—The largest attendance ever recorded at Fenway (September 22, 1935), for a twin bill with the Yankees. This was before fire laws and AL rules prevented such overcrowding.

.872—Smoky Joe Wood's winning percentage in 1912. He won 34 games and lost five. His ERA was a microscopic 1.91.

192—The number of wins Cy Young had as a member of the Boston Red Sox. He had 511 in his major league career.

316—The number of losses by Cy Young in his career—a major league record.

$3,500—The amount the Boston Americans paid to lure Cy Young from the St. Louis Cardinals in 1901.

2—The number of no-hitters pitched by Dutch Leonard (in 1916 vs. St. Louis and 1918 vs. Detroit).

2—Number of games Carl Mays won in a double-header against the Philadelphia Athletics at Fenway on August 30, 1918, the same day Ted Williams was born. Mays won the opener 12–0 and the nightcap 4–1, his 20th and 21st wins of the season.

29⅔—The then-record number of consecutive scoreless innings pitched by Babe Ruth in the 1916 and 1918 World Series. Ruth's daughter, Julia Ruth Stevens, claims it was his proudest achievement.

11—The league-leading home-run total by Babe Ruth in 1918. The rest of the team had four. Ruth also contributed a 13–7 mound record that year.

21—Smoky Joe Wood's age when he pitched a no-hitter against the St. Louis Browns on July 29, 1911.

29—The number of consecutive games combined that Smoky Joe and Walter "Big Train" Johnson had won going into their classic duel on September 6, 1912. Wood won the game 1–0.

and his record was 19–5 in only 25 starts, 17 of which were complete games, with seven of those being shutouts (he also notched three saves that year). In 1915 his ERA *ballooned* to a somewhat more mortal 2.36, but he still held enemy batters to a collective .208 average.

TOP TEN

Lowest Red Sox Single-Season ERAs

	Name	Year	ERA
1.	Dutch Leonard	1914	0.96
2.	Cy Young	1908	1.26
3.	Smoky Joe Wood	1915	1.49
4.	Ray Collins	1910	1.62t
	Cy Young	1901	1.62t
6.	Ernie Shore	1915	1.64
7.	Smoky Joe Wood	1910	1.68
8.	Rube Foster	1914	1.70
9.	Pedro Martinez	2000	1.74t
	Carl Mays	1917	1.74t

Tex Hughson: The Long, Tall Texan

He was a right-handed power pitcher who developed an arsenal of other baffling pitches to add to his blazing fastball, wore No. 21, played for the Boston Red Sox, and hailed from Texas. In fact, he pitched for the University of Texas Longhorns before coming to the majors. Oh yeah, and he left the Red Sox due to problems with the front office. Sound familiar?

No, it's not "Rocket" Roger Clemens we're speaking of, but tall, handsome Cecil "Tex" Hughson, who pitched for the Red Sox from 1941 to 1949. Hughson put together a 96–54 major league record and led the American League in wins and strikeouts in 1942, with a record of 22–6 and 113 Ks. Like Clemens, the three-time All-Star often found himself in highly anticipated duels with the best pitchers of the day. His clashes with Hal Newhouser and Bob Feller were instant classics.

Hughson pitched the game that clinched the American League pennant for the Boston Red Sox in 1946, a 1–0 shutout in which the only run came on a Ted Williams inside-the-park homer.

Ellis Kinder

Ellis Kinder was a great relief pitcher for the Boston Red Sox of the late '40s to middle '50s. In fact, the man they called "Old Folks" was the equivalent of today's closers. Unfortunately, he closed as many bars as he did ballgames, often drinking until the wee small hours before that day's game. He was sometimes still inebriated while on the mound, and on at least one occasion had to be removed from a game because he was hung over and vomiting. "Ellis was a great pitcher," says Mel Parnell. "He had one of the best changes of pace in baseball. He lived kind of tough, but when he got on a ballfield he was a great one. In New York one time he was out all night, and I was going out and he was coming in. And he still pitched a hell of a game. He was superhuman, really. We always claimed he had a rubber arm....He could throw all day, and he didn't take many pitches to warm up, either. He was a hell of a pitcher in my book, and I'm sure the batters who faced him would say the same."

Greg Harris: Switch-Pitcher

Greg Harris was a right-handed pitcher for the Boston Red Sox from 1989 to 1994. Or was he? He was a northpaw who wanted to pitch southpaw, and but for the objections of then General Manager Lou Gorman, he would have. Gorman thought that such an act would represent a "mockery" of the game of baseball and put the kibosh on the idea. Harris was an ambidextrous pitcher, and he had a dream scenario worked out in his mind. He wanted to be on the mound when a dangerous left-handed batter came to the plate. He then wanted to switch his glove to his right hand and pitch left-handed to the batter. Switch-hitters do it all the time. Why not pitchers?

TRIVIA

How high is the Green Monster?

Answers to the trivia questions are on pages 175–176.

IF ONLY . . . The Boston American League franchise had kept one of their early names. New York Yankees fans would be torn apart by the patriotic dilemma of whether or not to chant "Americans suck!" For that matter, such profanities hurled at Puritans might have given even those rude New Yorkers pause.

TRIVIA

Which two pitchers share the Red Sox record for career wins with 192?

Answers to the trivia questions are on pages 175–176.

Pitching Coach Rich Gale was willing to give it a try on one condition. "It wouldn't be done as a lark or a joke," he told Nick Cafardo of the *Globe* in 1992. "If we're going to do it, he'd have to get his throwing in and be physically prepared to do it. If you've got one left-handed hitter in the middle of four or five right-handers, I don't see anything wrong with letting him throw [left-handed]." Of course, it does conjure up one rather perplexing scenario: What happens if a switch-pitcher faces a switch-hitter? The at-bat might never end as the two keep altering from one side to the other.

Crash and Turn: The Fall and (Eventual) Rise of the Red Sox

Baseball Depression Hits Boston

The Ruthless Red Sox were now destined to wander in the baseball wilderness for untold years, and the teams of the 1920s and early 1930s were eminently forgettable.

The Red Sox greeted the new decade by finishing fifth in 1920 and 1921 and then going downhill. They finished dead last in 1922, 1923, 1925, 1926, 1927, 1928, and 1929, making the stock market crash look mild by comparison. In fact, long after the Great Depression was officially over, the real *depression* lingered for Red Sox fans.

And they earned their last-place finishes. The 1923 squad had the worst batting average, worst fielding percentage, and worst ERA in the junior circuit.

The dirty '30s began with the Red Sox finishing dead last again in 1930. They also came in last in 1932, losing a disgraceful 111 games and finishing so far out of first place—64 games!—that they couldn't see first without a good pair of binoculars. Then, just as they were beginning to develop mold from basement-dwelling, a millionaire named Tom Yawkey came along to revive the franchise and restore baseball to its proper place in Boston.

The Yawkey Years

In February 1933 Thomas Austin Yawkey, a 30-year-old heir to a fortune in pulp and paper and mining ventures, purchased the Red Sox. They were a bargain-basement organization, with the emphasis on "basement." The previous year's last-place team drew just a little more than two thousand fans per game, a number hard to imagine today, when fans would pay almost anything to get into Fenway Park, and crowds cue up for a chance to buy a Rem Dawg at Jerry Remy's hot dog stand.

Unlike Frazee, Yawkey lived and breathed baseball. And he was not afraid to spend money—even in the midst of the Depression—to make his Red Sox respectable once again. He raided the powerful Philadelphia Athletics to get Lefty Grove, Jimmie Foxx, Doc Cramer, and other notables; he obtained Rick Ferrell from the St. Louis Browns; George Pipgras and Billy Werber came over from the Yankees; and Wes Ferrell, Rick's brother, soon followed from the Cleveland Indians. Then, in a stunning move, Yawkey brought in Joe Cronin from the Washington Senators for $250,000.

Tom Yawkey, shown here with Red Sox Manager Joe Cronin (right) during the 1946 World Series, bought the Red Sox in 1933 and owned them until the day he died in 1976. He was inducted into baseball's Hall of Fame in 1980.

TOP TEN

Red Sox Single-Season Losses for Pitchers

	Name	Year	Losses
1.	Red Ruffing	1928	25
2.	Red Ruffing	1929	22
3.	Bill Dineen	1902	21†
	Joe Harris	1906	21†
	Cy Young	1906	21†
	Slim Harriss	1927	21†
7.	Sam ("Sad Sam") Jones	1919	20†
	Howard Ehmke	1925	20†
	Milt Gaston	1930	20†
	Jack Russell	1930	20†

After buying stars for several years without dramatic results, Yawkey concluded that this was not the way to win. He needed young players who could be groomed in the Red Sox system from the minor leagues to the big leagues. He created an extensive farm system based on the Yankees model. He turned his scouts loose with instructions to beat the bushes for young talent, and it was here that Yawkey finally started to turn things around for the Red Sox. He had General Manager Eddie Collins scout and sign future Hall of Famers Ted Williams and Bobby Doerr to bolster his veteran lineup. The Sox scouted and signed Tex Hughson, Boo Ferriss, Johnny Pesky, Dom DiMaggio, and Mickey Harris. They were now poised to be legitimate contenders for league honors.

Unfortunately, the Yankees played in the same league.

TRIVIA

Which Red Sox player holds the team record for the most homers in a single season?

a) Babe Ruth
b) Ted Williams
c) Jimmie Foxx
d) Carl Yastrzemski
e) Jim Rice
f) Manny Ramirez

Answers to the trivia questions are on pages 175–176.

Jimmie Foxx:
The Beast of Boston

Jimmie Foxx doesn't get as much attention as he should. Everyone knows about Ruth and Gehrig, Williams and DiMaggio, but Foxx was stronger than any of them. Ted Williams once said that, in comparison to Jimmie Foxx, he "felt weak." He went on to say that "if anyone was ever capable of tearing the cover off the ball, it would be Double X." Like a maestro whose practiced ear picks up every nuance of an orchestral performance, Ted could pick out a Foxx home run without even seeing it. "It sounded like cherry bombs when Foxx hit them...like firecrackers," he said with the respect of a fellow slugger. Yankees catcher Bill Dickey seconded Ted's assessment. "If I were catching blindfolded, I'd always know when it was Foxx who connected," said Dickey. "He hit the ball harder than anyone else."

For many years, Foxx was touted to displace Babe Ruth as baseball's home-run king, but the soft-spoken Maryland native didn't have the burning desire to do so. "If I had broken Ruth's record, it wouldn't have made any difference," he once said. "Oh, it might have put a few more dollars in my pocket, but there was only one Ruth."

Fellow players stood in awe of Foxx, especially pitchers. "He had muscles in his hair," claimed Lefty Gomez. When asked how he would pitch to the man known as "the Beast," he admitted that he'd "rather not pitch to him at all."

When Foxx arrived in Boston in 1936, he had already hit more than 300 home runs (302) as a member of the Philadelphia Athletics, including a Ruthian 58 in 1932, and had led the American League three times. He showed no signs of slowing down when he arrived at Fenway. During his six full years in Beantown, he was selected to the All-Star team every year. His debut season in Boston (1936) saw him hit 41 homers, followed by 36, 50, a league-leading 35, 36, and 19.

In six and one-half seasons for the Red Sox in the '30s and early '40s, slugger Jimmie Foxx, who had played on three Philadelphia Athletics World Series teams before joining Boston, hit 222 home runs and led the league in batting with a .349 average in 1938.

Memorable Red Sox Quotes

1. "Why not us?" —Curt Schilling, uttering the war cry of the 2004 Red Sox
2. "When everyone in the ballpark knows you're going to steal against Rivera, it's pretty tough." —Dave Roberts, in the locker room after doing just that to spark the Red Sox to a win in Game 4 of the 2004 ALCS
3. "All I want out of life is to be able to walk down the street and have people say 'There goes the greatest hitter who ever lived.'" —Ted Williams
4. "Tied." —Bill Lee, when asked before Game 7 of the 1975 World Series how he would characterize the series so far
5. "Yes, but you don't have to go into the stands and play your foul balls." —Golfer Sam Snead responding to Ted Williams' claim that hitting a baseball was tougher than hitting a golf ball
6. "Babe Ruth gave me more trouble than any other left-handed pitcher." —Ty Cobb
7. "Joe Cronin was the best clutch hitter I ever saw, and that includes Ty Cobb." —Connie Mack
8. "I could always hit, but not like Ted Williams. He was in a class by himself." —Tris Speaker
9. "We need to cowboy up!" —Kevin Millar, coining a new war cry for Red Sox Nation
10. "As long as I've got my cup on." —Jimy Williams, former Red Sox manager, when asked if reporters could talk to him

Foxx became a heavy drinker ("a low-ball hitter and a highball drinker," said teammates) but was always popular with the fans and his teammates. Williams, who played with him from 1939 to 1942, referred to him as "a big old lovable bear of a guy."

Pitchers feared Foxx like no other hitter, as evidenced by the six walks he was accorded on June 16, 1938.

Birdie Tebbetts: Class Act

Former Red Sox catcher Birdie Tebbetts was once calling pitches in a game with the Chicago White Sox. The home-plate umpire was Red Ormsby, who had been gassed in World War I and suffered from occasional blurred vision and dizzy spells. On this particular day, Ormsby was not at all well. Just before the first pitch was delivered, he tapped on Tebbetts' shoulder and said, "Birdie, I'm sick. Call the pitches for me for awhile." Tebbetts didn't miss a beat or embarrass the umpire by even turning around to face him. "Okay, Red," he replied. What followed was bizarre and heartwarming at the same time. The pitcher wound and threw the first pitch. "Ball," whispered Tebbetts, and "BALL!" echoed Ormsby in his best umpire's shout. "Ball two," said Tebbetts softly as the second pitch arrived low and outside. "BALL!" said the ump. "Strike," whispered Tebbetts on the next delivery and "STRIKE!" repeated Ormsby loudly while signaling with his right arm. This went on for the full half-inning, with Tebbetts calling balls and strikes fairly for his own pitcher. But it didn't stop there. Before Tebbetts left for the dugout, he explained the situation to his White Sox counterpart, Mike Tresh, and this odd and noble act was extended for two more outs until Ormsby announced himself ready to resume his duties. Tebbetts was asked about how the hitters reacted to the opposing catcher calling the game. "They understood," he said.

TOP TEN

Stupid Statements by a Red Sox Manager or Executive

1. "I do not mind saying I think the Yankees are making a gamble. The Red Sox can now go into the market and buy other players and have a stronger and better team than if Ruth had remained with us." —Red Sox owner Harry Frazee on the sale of Ruth to New York in 1920

2. "I would be the laughingstock of the league if I took the best left-handed pitcher in the league and put him in the outfield." —Ed Barrow, Red Sox manager

3. "Get that nigger off the field." —unidentified Red Sox executive, as Jackie Robinson was being given a tryout at Fenway Park

4. "Clemens is in the twilight of his career." —Red Sox General Manager Dan Duquette, following the 1996 season. Duquette dealt Clemens to Toronto, where he won two Cy Young Awards. He then helped the Yankees to win World Series titles in 1999 and 2000. He won another Cy Young in 2001, a year in which he posted a 20–3 record. After briefly retiring, Clemens came back to record an 18–4 mark with his hometown Houston Astros and win his seventh Cy Young. In 2005 he posted a 1.87 ERA and 13–8 record in helping the Astros to the World Series.

5. "Kid, I've changed my mind. I'm going with the right-hander." —Joe McCarthy to Mel Parnell, before the disastrous 1948 playoff game against Cleveland. McCarthy chose to start Denny Galehouse instead of the Boston ace. Galehouse had been 8–8 that year with a 4.00 ERA; Parnell was 15–8 with a 3.14 ERA. The Red Sox lost the game 8–3, and Galehouse was gone by the fourth inning.

6. "He has good hands and he was running well today [other reports quote him as saying 'he was hobbling well

today']." —Red Sox Manager John McNamara, after Game 6 of the World Series, explaining why he left a hobbled Bill Buckner at first base instead of inserting Dave Stapleton into the lineup as a defensive replacement. The unfortunate Buckner allowed the Mets to rally and win the game and eventually the World Series.

7. "Next to Jim Rice, he's the strongest guy on the team, maybe in all of baseball, but he's got the balls of a female cow." —Bovine-challenged former Red Sox manager Don Zimmer, describing right fielder Dwight Evans

8. "Why, I wouldn't pay one of my actors that much." —Red Sox owner Harry Frazee in 1919, on Babe Ruth's outrageous demand for $10,000

9. "If Grady Little isn't back with the Red Sox, I'll be another ghost fully capable of haunting." —Grady Little, after leaving Pedro Martinez in Game 7 of the 2003 NLCS, but before being fired

10. "Ted, I think you ought to quit....Why don't you just wrap it up?" Red Sox owner Tom Yawkey to Ted Williams, after his injury-plagued 1959 season, the worst year of his career (.254 batting average and 10 homers); Ted came back in 1960 to hit .316 with 29 homers, including one in his final at-bat

Roger Clemens spent 13 years as the ace of the Boston staff. As a Red Sox player, he led the league in ERA four times and strikeouts three times, winning the Cy Young Award three times as well.

Ted Williams:
The Five Senses

If Babe Ruth is the patron saint of the New York Yankees, Ted Williams is the deity who will forever rule over the firmament of Red Sox Nation. Despite his infamous battles with the Boston media and fans, Williams once said that he would never have left the Red Sox because of his loyalty to owner Tom Yawkey: "The way I felt about Tom Yawkey, I could never have played for anyone else. And I loved Eddie Collins and Joe Cronin." Ted's loyalty made him a lifelong member of the Red Sox. When he signed on to the Sox, he did so, for better or for worse, for his entire career.

Indeed, if Ted had gone to New York, it would have made Ruth's departure pale in comparison. Ted was an icon. He *was* the Boston Red Sox.

Where do you start? Ted was one of a kind, the best hitter in baseball history. This does not mean he hit more home runs than anyone else, or had the highest batting average. It just means he was a genius with a bat and used it like a maestro uses his baton. He hit 521 home runs without the benefit of juice (steroids) or juiced balls, and while sacrificing almost five prime years to service in World War II and Korea. He batted .344 lifetime without sacrificing power. He was the most respected hitter within a hitting fraternity that included names like Joe DiMaggio, Mickey Mantle, Hank Greenberg, and Stan Musial. Ted was the last man to hit .400 in a major league season (.406 in 1941) and ended his career the way every player dreams of doing, with a home run in his final at-bat.

Everyone knows that Ted Williams had a keen batting eye. The Navy doctor who checked his eyesight on enlistment in 1942 declared that he had 20-10 vision. Stories circulated that he could read a phonograph record label while it was still spinning and could see ducks approaching before fellow hunters. His ability to discern a ball from a strike is legendary

Perhaps the game's best pure hitter, Ted Williams, here collecting a hit against the Tigers in a 1954 doubleheader in which he had eight hits on the day, spent his entire 19-year career with the Red Sox. He led the American League in hitting six times, home runs four times, doubles twice, RBIs four times, and walks eight times. He's also the last man to hit .400 in a season, which he did in 1941 when he hit .406.

and often gave him the benefit of the doubt when umpires had to make close calls. "They always claim that great hitters got a fourth strike," said Hank Aaron. "Ted didn't get no fourth strike, it was just that he knew where the strike zone was, and he wouldn't swing at anything outside of the strike zone." His association with major league arbiters was one of mutual respect. Umpires loved Ted because he never embarrassed them by arguing calls.

Ted did not like to hear the exaggerations about his "superhuman vision," believing that it detracted from the hours of work and dedication

TOP TEN

Red Sox Single-Season Batting Averages

	Name	Average	Year
1.	Ted Williams	.406	1941
2.	Ted Williams	.388	1957
3.	Tris Speaker	.383	1912
4.	Nomar Garciaparra	.372	2000
5.	Ted Williams	.369	1948
6.	Wade Boggs	.368	1985
7.	Wade Boggs	.366	1988
8.	Tris Speaker	.363	1913
9.	Wade Boggs	.363	1987
10.	Wade Boggs	.361	1983

he put into his craft. Opposing pitchers were convinced that Ted actually saw the stitches on approaching pitches and instantly computed what the ball was going to do. He claimed that the reason he saw things so well was due to his "intensity." He wanted to see them well and concentrated on doing so. "It takes a hell of a lot more than good eyesight to hit .400 in the major leagues," he once said. "I hurt my eye when I was a kid, and there were plenty of times when I couldn't see well that day and *still* get three hits." But he also admitted, "It would be impossible to become a great hitter without it." Ted once claimed that home plate at Fenway was out of line. Everyone laughed at the suggestion. When they checked it the next day, Ted was proven correct.

As for his ears, Ted could pick out a single shouted insult from what he called a "leather-lunged fan" amidst a chorus of cheers at Fenway Park. Hank Aaron was once amazed at Ted's auditory aplomb. "The first time I saw Ted was when I played an exhibition game against the Red Sox and I hit a home run off Ike Delock," recalls Hammerin' Hank. "Ted said 'Boy, I was in the clubhouse and I heard the crack of the bat and I said—Lord, I've gotta go look!—and I knew immediately that it was one of the longest home runs that was ever hit at the Red Sox training site at Sarasota.' I'd always heard about Ted Williams' baseball savvy, and right then and there, I could appreciate exactly what he meant. No wonder Ted's name has been synonymous with hitting."

Ted could tell a Foxx home run from a Mantle home run from a Killebrew home run the way a wine connoisseur could spot a particular vintage of fine wine.

Ted's sense of touch is legendary. A bat had to have the right feel, the right weight. He used to make occasional pilgrimages to the Louisville Slugger factory to pick out just the right wood for his bats. He used to use a bone to harden the grain in his bats. "I treated them like babies," he said in his biography *My Turn at Bat*.

As part of a *Sports Illustrated* cover story in 1986, Williams was united with two of the best hitters of the day: Don Mattingly of the New York Yankees and Wade Boggs of the Red Sox. During the course of their discussion, Williams dropped a bombshell, stating that a few times in his career, he actually smelled wood burning when he barely fouled off a fastball. Boggs and Mattingly smelled a rat, but Williams was serious. The bat speed that would have to be generated for such an act of spontaneous combustion is mind-boggling.

Taste is not a prerequisite to great hitting, but Ted's prodigious taste for food was in direct proportion to his prodigious hitting feats. In 1946 Mel Webb reported in the *Boston Globe* that Williams consumed the following: three shrimp cocktails, three cups of fish chowder, one 1¼"-thick steak, ten rolls, one pound of butter, two orders of string beans, two 2½-pound broiled lobsters, one chef's salad, three ice creams with chocolate sauce, and "an indeterminate amount" of iced tea. Joe Falls, the brilliant Detroit columnist and friend of Ted Williams (yes, Ted did have friends in the media!), tells of late-night forays he and Ted made in search of ice cream. "Ted takes me to dinner and he does the ordering. You've gotta eat what he eats because you don't get a chance to order. So I ate what he ate. Then the old chocoholic took me to Howard Johnson's and orders a fudge brownie with chocolate ice cream on it and chocolate sauce on top of all of that and I had to eat one, too. I was repulsed but I had to eat it." His love of ice cream reportedly once took him to a restaurant across the street from Fenway between games of a double-header, still wearing his Red Sox uniform.

TRIVIA

Ted Williams won Triple Crowns in 1942 and 1947 and yet was not selected the league MVP either year. Who beat him?

Answers to the trivia questions are on pages 175–176.

TOP TEN

Quotes about Ted Williams from Fellow Hall of Famers

1. "He was an Einstein with the bat. Precise, mechanically perfect, every swing beautifully executed. He's my idol." —Mickey Mantle

2. "He studied hitting the way a broker studies the stock market, and could spot at a glance the mistakes that others couldn't see in a week." —Carl Yastrzemski

3. "I went to watch the Browns play the Red Sox. I go there early and it had to be the 10 or 15 most wonderful moments of my life, watching Ted Williams in batting practice. This has got to be the most perfect batting swing in all baseball history." —Willie Mays

4. "Ted was a once-in-a generation hitter, the best of our time, without question." —Stan Musial

5. "He was the best I ever saw. There was nobody like him." —Joe DiMaggio

6. "Ted is one of the greatest natural hitters I've ever seen. If he'd hit to left field, he'd break up that [Boudreau] shift and break every record in the book. He'd hit .500." —Ty Cobb

7. "Williams was just out of this world as a hitter. The best of them all." —Tris Speaker

8. "I admired Ted tremendously. He was one of the greatest to put on a uniform, to pick up a bat....Ted was a better hitter than I was. Ted hit .400 and some of the things that he did not accomplish were only because he lost five years to the service. He could have eclipsed Babe Ruth's home-run record. He probably would have hit .400 again." —Hank Aaron

9. "There's no doubt in my mind that he was the greatest hitter baseball's ever had. There's no way you could throw a fastball by Ted." —Bob Feller

10. "Williams was one of my three childhood idols. Jackie Robinson and Nellie Fox are the others." —Joe Morgan

In the 1946 All-Star Game in Boston, Ted Williams, just back from the war, had the National League waving white flags of surrender with an offensive barrage that was the talk of baseball. In the first inning, Ted drew a base on balls from NL starter Claude Passeau (off of whom Williams had homered to win the 1941 mid-summer classic). Ted hit a home run next time up, this time against Kirby Higbe. He then singled off Higbe; then another one-base hit off Ewell Blackwell. Finally, with two men on base in the bottom of the eighth inning, Ted stepped to the plate against a man named Rip Sewell. Sewell was famous for his "eephus" pitch that arrived at the plate in a dramatic arc, almost like the delivery of an overweight ace from your neighborhood slow-pitch softball league. Ted swung and missed the first pitch, a big grin of surprise and delight on his face. Popular conjecture

TRIVIA

What Red Sox outfield has been termed the "most high-strung" in baseball history?

Answers to the trivia questions are on pages 175–176.

had it that no one could homer off such a pitch since the batter had to provide all the power. On the next delivery, Ted took a couple of jump steps toward the mound and pounded the ball into the right-field bullpen. (Ted later said that the homer could actually have been nullified because technically he was out of the batter's box.) He homered once more to round out his day—giving him two homers, two singles, a walk, four runs scored, and five RBIs. "That was the first homer ever hit off that pitch," said Sewell later. "I still don't believe it."

Ted has legions of admirers on and off the field, but don't count former 30-game winner Denny McLain among them. McLain pitched for Williams when he was a member of the Washington Senators on the downward slope of his career. Said McLain in his autobiography *Nobody's Perfect*: "Every manager I ever played under was human, except for Theodore Samuel Williams. Whatever I have done wrong in life, I atoned for it in the one season I spent playing for Ted Williams in Washington."

In 1958 Red Sox General Manager Joe Cronin estimated that Ted Williams was personally responsible for approximately 50 percent of the total Red Sox gate. Ted was making $125,000 at the time. Also in 1957 Ted raised $550,000 as chairman of the Jimmy Fund, a charity for children's cancer

TOP TEN

Quotes from Ted Williams about Red Sox Players

1. "He wasn't as smart as he should have been and he never knew when he was doing it right...[but Bobby Doerr] said he had the best single year he'd ever seen, and Bobby played with *me* for 10 years!" —Ted on Carl Yastrzemski

2. "He hit as if he had two strikes on him all the time. He was strong as a bull, but he was swinging when he left the bench." —Ted on Jim Rice

3. "If production is the yardstick of the great hitter, and I sincerely believe that it is, then Jimmie Foxx must be the Henry Ford of hitters. He hit balls out of sight." —Ted on Jimmie Foxx

4. "I personally think that Babe Ruth has to be the greatest player of all time. He was not only a great slugger—the greatest slugger the game has ever seen or ever will see—but he was also a great pitcher...one of the greatest of his time." —Ted on Babe Ruth

5. "When I watch Dwight Evans at the plate, it makes me want to vomit." —Ted on Dwight Evans and his fidgeting at the plate

6. "He's as good a young player as anyone I've seen come into the big leagues. He went to Georgia Tech where he was on the Dean's List and when I finished talking with him, I felt I was on the Dean's List of hitting. I asked him my usual questions about all aspects of hitting...and he knew everything. He's really a brilliant kid." —Ted on Nomar Garciaparra

7. "If he's selective, he can hit down the left-field line and he can hit down the right-field line; but if he's fooled, the Babe himself can't hit the ball....He seems to have a plan when he comes to the plate, unlike many of today's young hitters." —Ted on Mo Vaughn

8. "Boggs is a very smart hitter. He makes the pitchers pitch. If he's fooled, he doesn't fool with the pitch. When he's got two strikes, he'll go inside-out, inside-out. He has that much facility hitting with two strikes....In batting practice, Boggs will put a hell of a long-ball show on for you in the bleachers, but in a game—phip! phip! phip!—he tries to spray the ball."
—Ted on Wade Boggs

9. "Tris Speaker was capable of doing a little bit more as a hitter than he did, because he played almost 10 years in the lively ball era and still didn't hit as many home runs as he should have....Home runs were not his priority, I guess. He was considered to be in the aristocracy of baseball, and in my mind he belongs in the aristocracy of hitters." —Ted on Tris Speaker

10. "Come on, you blond bum! I don't want to stand out here in the sun all day." —Ted, on first base, yelling to Jackie Jensen at the plate (Jensen homered on the next pitch)

research. On August 17 of that year, the Splendid Splinter made a pitch for the Fund on *The Ed Sullivan Show*: "Yesterday's base hits don't win today's games," said Ted. "There is a lot of research to be done in the hope of conquering one of the worst disasters which has afflicted mankind."

Jimmy Piersall, the talented but troubled center fielder who played alongside Ted for many years, was much more media-friendly than his outfield neighbor:

"He knows I like the newspapermen and he gets on me about it," Piersall said in 1957. "I give it back to him because I like to needle him. One time I was in the dugout in Baltimore talking with a bunch of writers and Ted said to me, 'Why don't you kiss all those guys, you're so crazy about them?' So I did. I got up and kissed all the writers." Piersall had some sympathy for Ted's stand against the working press, however. "Some writers could be pretty mean," he admitted. "A guy in Washington quoted me that I should get paid half of Ted's salary for covering his territory.

I never said it. I told Ted I never said it, and he said, 'Well, you tell him.' But it was a writer who never comes to the park. I don't even know what he looks like. He said things about Nixon and White [too]. They'd strangle him if he ever showed up."

When Ted had built a reputation as the most feared and respected hitter in the game, he faced a fresh-faced rookie pitcher from the Washington Senators named Pedro Ramos. Ramos struck Ted out. After the game, Ramos came into the Red Sox clubhouse and shyly asked Ted to autograph the ball with which he had recorded the strikeout. Ted exploded. "Are you f*cking nuts? I'm not signing any goddamn ball I struck out on!" he roared. Ramos, who was a huge fan of Ted's, was crushed and began to retreat toward the door. Seeing this, Ted relented and signed the ball, congratulating the young hurler and wishing him well. The next time they met, Ted hit a monster home run off Ramos that traveled far into the right-field bleachers at Fenway. As he rounded first, a grinning Ted slowed down a bit and yelled at the precocious rookie, "I'll sign that son of a bitch, too, if you can ever find it."

When Ted took over as manager of the Washington Senators (which later became the Texas Rangers) in 1969, the entire writing fraternity of America waited for the first clash with the media. "Ted Williams could become the first manager to throw a baseball writer across the Potomac," suggested New York columnist Dick Young. Young continued, "Did you ever notice that the newspaper guys who boast about being buddy-buddy with Ted Williams are the ones who see him once a year. I could get along with my wife if I saw her once a year."

By the NUMBERS

3—Number of wives that Ted Williams had.

4½—The number of years lost by Ted Williams due to service in World War II and Korea.

1—Number of players to pinch-hit for Ted Williams. His name was Carroll Hardy.

1—Number of points Triple Crown winner Ted Williams lost the MVP by in 1947 (to Joe DiMaggio)—one sportswriter completely left Williams off his list of top 10 players.

Ted Williams struck out only 709 times in his entire career while hitting 521 home runs.

Ted once came face to face with another Ted Williams—this one a pitcher! In the spring of 1981, a young pitcher named Ted Williams Kromy was training in Florida with the Minnesota Twins. Kromy had read Ted's autobiography, *My Turn At Bat*, and his book on hitting, *The Science of Hitting*, and, in fact, knew almost everything there was to know about his namesake. He even knew that Ted had been a pitcher for a while in San Diego. His father, a former Triple A player with Baltimore had seen the original Teddy Ballgame play in Minneapolis and was impressed enough to give his son the name. The young pitcher met Ted during a Twins–Red Sox exhibition at Winter Haven, Florida. Ted's reaction was predictable for someone who made his living in out-foxing moundsmen. "You're a pitcher, huh?" he said in mock disgust. He went on to wish him luck.

TRIVIA

What is the Boudreau Shift and when was it first used?

Answers to the trivia questions are on pages 175–176.

Ted's last at-bat is one of the most discussed and analyzed home runs in history. Everyone from John Updike on down the writing food chain has written about it. Let's hear what Ted had to say about the dramatic poke in his autobiography, *My Turn At Bat*: "There were only 10,454 people in Fenway Park that day, but they reacted like nothing I had ever heard. I mean they really put it on. They cheered like hell, and as I came around, the cheering grew louder and louder. I thought about tipping my hat, you're damn right I did, and for a moment I was torn, but by the time I got to second base I knew I couldn't do it."

Brooks Robinson, who was playing third for the Orioles that day, claims that watching the home run was "one of my greatest thrills in baseball," and that it gave him "chills." It remains the greatest exit in the history of any sport.

Johnny Pesky: Mr. Red Sox

Johnny Pesky is Mr. Red Sox. He has served the team as a player, manager, coach, instructor, announcer, and mentor. He has helped Wade Boggs become a Gold Glove third baseman by hitting countless ground balls to him, and has provided a father figure to countless fresh rookies.

Of course, he is best known for getting on base so that Ted Williams could drive him in. Pesky did just that from day one, collecting 205 hits in his first year, a Red Sox rookie record. It also led the league.

Despite his many accomplishments, Pesky's name will forever be connected with a single play from the seventh game of the 1946 World Series against St. Louis. The two teams were tied three games apiece in St. Louis. With two out in the bottom of the eighth and the score tied 3–3, Enos Slaughter was on first base. Harry Walker hit a dying-quail double into center, and Slaughter, who had been off on contact, was hell bent on scoring. The ball was relayed to shortstop Pesky, who had his back turned to the plate and didn't realize that Slaughter was going home. Pesky's relay was late, and the Cardinals won the game and the Series. The accusation, most unfair, has always been that "Pesky held the ball." In actual fact, if Dom DiMaggio, who had pulled a muscle earlier in the game, had been in centerfield instead of cumbersome Leon Culberson, who threw the ball in on a slow arc, the result might have been quite different.

Pesky's Pole, the foul pole down the right-field line, stands as a constant reminder of one of the Red Sox's most essential players. The pole was so dubbed by Mel Parnell after a game in which Pesky hit a home run past it that barely went fair. In fact, Pesky hit only a handful of such homers, but the name stuck.

The heart of the great 1950 Red Sox offense, which hit .300 as a team and led the league in runs scored, stands on the top step of the dugout the next year to honor second baseman Bobby Doerr (center), who was retiring because of back problems. The others, from left: third baseman Johnny Pesky, center fielder Dom DiMaggio, Manager Steve O'Neil, and Ted Williams.

Johnny Pesky is not ashamed to have been a table-setter for his friend and teammate Ted Williams, but lest he ever forget his supporting role, columnist Joe Falls of the *Detroit Free Press* and *The Sporting News* was there to keep him humble. When Pesky was managing the Red Sox, Falls would sneak up behind him and say, "How was it hitting ahead of Ted Williams?" This was Falls' form of greeting whenever he saw his old friend. "I knew it would get to him," he recalled years later. "Through his whole career he heard how lucky he was to bat ahead of the Great Man. The pitchers didn't want anyone on base when Williams came up and so rather than take the chance of walking Pesky, they'd come over the plate with the ball and let him hit it." Falls knew that Pesky was well aware of the little game he was playing. "[After a while] he wouldn't even turn around to look at me. He'd merely say 'It was great hitting ahead of Williams. Fast balls, waist high.'"

Many Boston Red Sox observers, notably the *Globe*'s Steve Buckley, feel that Pesky's No. 6 should be retired. Who could argue? He is, after all, Mr. Red Sox.

TOP TEN

Seasons to Savor

1. 2004—The Red Sox win it all. No need to explain
2. 1941—Ted Williams batted .406 and remains the last player in either league to accomplish that feat. He also led the American league in home runs with 37 to capture two-thirds of the Triple Crown. He ended up with 120 RBIs. He was also tops in on-base percentage with .553, slugging percentage with .735, runs scored with 135, and walks, with 147. It was a season in which he had to vie with the Yankees Joe DiMaggio for media attention, as Joe was putting together a 56-game hitting streak.
3. 1946—With the war finally over and America hungry for baseball, the Red Sox won the American League pennant and faced the St. Louis Cardinals in the World Series. Although they lost in seven games to the Cardinals, it looked like the first of many such World Series appearances for the Boston squad. Alas, it was not to be.
4. 1967—Carl Yastrzemski was a one-man wrecking crew. Not only did he capture the Triple Crown on the strength of 44 homers (tied with Harmon Killebrew), a .326 batting average, and 121 RBIs, he seemed to be a factor in virtually every Red Sox win, especially down the stretch when the Red Sox were battling for

the pennant. He made spectacular catches in left field, played caroms off the wall with the genius of a pool hustler, and prevented countless opposition runs with his accurate throws.

5. 1975—The Red Sox were doubly blessed when a pair of rookies named Jim Rice and Fred Lynn joined the lineup and helped lead the Red Sox to the AL pennant. The "Gold Dust Twins," as they were called, proceeded to tear the league apart, combining for 207 RBIs (Lynn had 105, Rice 102), 195 runs (Lynn with a league-best 103), 43 homers (Rice with 22, Lynn 21), and 349 hits. Lynn batted .331 and Rice .309.

6. 1986—The Red Sox had a year to remember, winning the AL pennant and coming within a strike of a World Series title against the Mets. Clemens was a key part of the Sox' success. On April 20, Roger struck out 20 members of the Seattle Mariners in a nine-inning game. The Rocket allowed only three hits and no walks. Dwight Evans provided the Red Sox runs, clouting a three-run homer in the 3–1 victory.

7. 1912—The Red Sox moved to Fenway Park, grabbed the AL pennant, and won their second World Series against the New York Giants, the team that refused to play "minor leaguers" in the canceled 1904 Series. Tris Speaker had his signature season, batting .383; and Smoky Joe Wood posted a 34–5 record. That's an .872 winning percentage, folks. His ERA was a microscopic 1.91.

8. 1918—Babe Ruth helped to lead the Red Sox to what would be their last world title in 86 years.

9. 2003—Close, oh so close, but still a wonderful season until the very end.

10. 1903—The Red Sox win the first-ever World Series, 5 games to 3, against the National League champion Pittsburgh Pirates. It would be the first of five championships for the Sox over the next 15 years—of course, it would also be the first of six over the next 101 years.

Tony Conigliaro: Promise Unfulfilled

The story of Tony Conigliaro is an American tragedy. The movie-star–handsome native of Revere, Massachusetts, was a star with seemingly unlimited potential. He had power, flair, charisma, and wholesome hometown appeal. Life should have held limitless potential for this young phenom. And then came that fateful day of August 18, 1967.

The Red Sox were playing the California Angels at Fenway Park. The Angels starting pitcher was Jack Hamilton, a right-hander who allowed 63 walks while striking out 74 for the Angels that year (he started the year with the Mets). He had only hit one batter all season long, just 12 in his six-year career. Conigliaro had singled his first time up. Tony C had a habit of crowding the plate and treating it as his own turf, practically daring pitchers to throw inside to move him back. In his young career he had already suffered four broken bones from being hit by pitches. But still he did not back off. Hamilton threw a fastball that sailed toward Tony's head. The young batter seemed to freeze like a deer in the headlights. At the last split second, his head jerked back and his helmet flew off, leaving his face totally exposed to the ball. There was a sickening thud as ball met flesh. Angels catcher Buck Rodgers was later to comment that it sounded like a bat striking a pumpkin full force. The next instant he was on the ground with players and coaches gathered around him. Fenway Park was silent.

Tony was rushed to the hospital. The fastball had broken his cheekbone. More ominously, it had severely damaged his eyesight. He ended up missing the entire 1968 season. It looked like the apparent tragedy would have a happy ending when he returned to the Red Sox in 1969, slugged 20 homers, and captured the Comeback Player of the Year Award. Even as late as 1970, he hit 36 home runs with 116 RBIs. Unknown to fans and even teammates, he was accomplishing these feats with only

Outfielder Tony Conigliaro was a local boy who joined the Red Sox in 1964 when he was just 19. He hit 104 home runs before his career was slowed down by a gruesome beaning to the eye that shelved him for nearly a season and a half. He was never quite the same player again and was out of baseball by the age of 30.

one fully functional eye. He was traded to the California Angels following the 1970 season, a trade that the Conigliaro family considered a betrayal. He retired in the middle of the 1971 campaign, only to attempt another comeback with the Red Sox in 1975. Alas, it was not to be. His major league career was over. Conigliaro finished his 876-game career with 166 homers, a small indication of what might have been.

In 1982 Tony C suffered a heart attack that left him in a coma for over a month. When he came out of the coma, there was hope that he might make a miracle recovery. Despite the prayers of all New England and the loving attention of his family, Tony Conigliaro died on February 24, 1990, at the age of 45. A little bit of New England died with him. He had been the centerpiece of a kind of baseball Camelot.

TRIVIA

What was the name of Tony Conigliaro's hit single (a hit in Boston at least)?

Answers to the trivia questions are on pages 175–176.

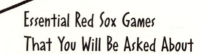

Essential Red Sox Games
That You Will Be Asked About

Here is the author's ranking of the 10 most significant Red Sox games:

1. October 27, 2004—World Series Game 4 vs. St. Louis
2. October 20, 2004—ALCS Game 7 vs. New York Yankees
3. October 21, 1975—World Series Game 6 vs. Cincinnati, Carlton Fisk homer
4. October 25, 1986—World Series Game 6 vs. New York Mets, Bill Buckner's error
5. October 16, 2003—ALCS Game 7 vs. Yankees, Aaron Boone game
6. October 2, 1978—AL East playoff vs. Yankees, "Bucky 'F*cking' Dent"
7. October 17–19, 2004—ALCS Games 4, 5, and 6 vs. Yankees—a three-way tie
8. October 12, 1986—ALCS Game 5 vs. California Angels, Dave "Hindu" Henderson's ninth-inning, go-ahead home run and eleventh-inning sac-fly, game-winning RBI
9. September 28, 1960—Ted Williams' final game, final at-bat, and final home run
10. April 29, 1986—Clemens' 20-K game vs. Seattle

Yaz

When Carl Yastrzemski stepped into Ted Williams' large shoes in left field at Fenway, no one expected that the rookie would single-handedly change Red Sox fortunes—and indeed he didn't, at least not right away. He toiled away from 1961 to 1967 before the Red Sox suddenly and miraculously became a contender. But it was Yaz who did it. Make no mistake about that. Give some credit to manager Dick Williams, sure. And a lot to young teammates such as Rico Petrocelli, Tony Conigliaro, and Jim Lonborg. But Yastrzemski is the man responsible for turning the franchise around and making the Red Sox the most envied franchise in North American professional sports today. Sorry, Yankees fans.

Despite having retired in 1983, the impact Yaz had is still being felt to this day. He changed the Bosox from a team with superstars, but no team concept, to a *team* in the best sense of the word.

Yastrzemski: From Unpronounceable to Unforgettable

In 1961 Carl Yastrzemski, the Polish son of a Long Island, New York, potato farmer, came to Boston and was given the unenviable, if not impossible, task of not only replacing Ted Williams in left field, but of replacing him in the batting order. The enormity of that challenge boggles the mind, and for the rest of his Hall of Fame career, Yaz would be compared with Ted. It was a comparison he could never win.

Ted was once asked by the author of this book to compare himself with his successor. His answer was honest, straightforward, and pretty accurate: "I think we should understand each other, you and I, well enough to know that I may make a statement that doesn't sound altogether complimentary to somebody, but it's a fact. *You* mentioned it! Hell, Yaz got a home run every 26 or 27 times at the plate. He's been up over four thousand more times than I have and has driven in only five more runs [1,844 to 1,839], hasn't hit as many home runs [Ted had 521, Yaz 452], and with his .285 average, he's hit 60 points less lifetime average than I did. I would be the very first to admit that Yaz was a great all-around player, but all you have to do is look at his offensive statistics." Brutal? Sure. But also fair. And finishing second to Ted Williams as the Boston Red Sox's greatest player isn't bad.

Ted would have been the first to admit that Yaz was perhaps a better all-around player than he was when fielding skills were evaluated.

Ted Williams was a baseball god. He was the sort of player—like Michael Jordon in basketball or Bobby Orr in hockey—that fans just sit back and admire. But they can't really identify with that level of greatness. It's almost as if they are a different species—thoroughbreds in a world of nags. Carl Yastrzemski was a superstar with whom everyone could identify. When he made his first trip to Fenway Park and met with owner Tom Yawkey, Yawkey was prepared to meet a player of Williams' physical stature. What he saw was a slight, 5'11" former shortstop who could hardly have impressed the world-weary owner who had watched guys like Foxx and Williams try, and fail, to win him a world championship.

In 1967 Yaz did everything that can be expected of a major league ballplayer. He fielded superbly, always threw to the right base, and ran the bases with the instincts and cunning of a hyperactive chess player. So at the end of the year, a year in which he captured the Triple Crown with a .326 batting average, 44 homers, and 121 RBIs—and had guided the Red Sox all the way to the seventh game of the World Series—it was only right and proper that Yastrzemski should be the unanimous choice as American League MVP. Instead, Carl received 19 of the possible 20 votes from writers. Columnist Arthur Daley, among many others, was embarrassed and outraged at the affront to common sense, calling the one contrary voter a "muddle-headed operative, who apparently has been looking at different ballgames all year."

When a young Carl Yastrzemski was first taken to Boston and given a tour of Fenway Park, he uttered four prophetic words. "I can hit here," he concluded.

By the NUMBERS **.326, 44, 121**—Carl Yastrzemski's Triple Crown numbers for batting average, home runs, and RBIs in 1967.

2—Number of regular left fielders for Red Sox from 1939 to 1983.

Yaz's years in Boston were not all marked with cheers and adulation. Like Ted Williams before him, he was often the target of boo birds—the "Raz Yaz" club—and they made his life miserable for a few seasons. On one occasion, when the denizens of the left-field line were really getting to him, he made a big show of removing large wads of cotton batting from his ears, instantly turning the jeers to cheers.

In 1968 pitching dominated the American League, and it looked as if the junior circuit would not produce a .300 hitter. George "Boomer" Scott recalled a conversation with Yastrzemski at midseason. "He made a believer out of me a long time ago. [Yaz] was looking at the paper at the batting leaders. Tony Oliva was leading the American League with a .298 average, but there were guys in the National League hitting .340 and .330. He was hitting about .270 at the time, and he said to me, 'It would be embarrassing for the American League not to have one .300 hitter, wouldn't it?' I said, 'Yeah.' There was about a month to go, and he went out and put on one of the greatest exhibitions I've ever seen, and he won the batting title with .301."

Detroit Tigers pitcher Mickey Lolich paid a visit to the White House in 1972 and was introduced to President Richard M. Nixon. Lolich tried to get some advice from the nation's top executive. "I notice where you occasionally help football teams with suggested plays," said Lolich. "Would you be good enough to tell me how to pitch to Carl Yastrzemski?" Nixon thought for a moment and replied, "Sliders, down and in." Since Lolich was a southpaw, the advice did not ring true, and the pitcher said so. "We don't exactly do it that way, Mr. President," he said politely. Maybe it was a case of right-wing advice not suited to a left-wing pitcher.

Dave O'Hara, for 50 (yes, 50) years, was the Associated Press' New England sports editor. During that time, he saw a lot of greats and not-so-greats come and go. One player stands out. "Let me tell you about Yastrzemski," he volunteered to George Whitney in *Diehard* in August 1992. "In 1978 I had a bat autographed by Henry Aaron and Eddie Matthews, the best right-left punch ever in baseball. *SI* [*Sports Illustrated*] wanted to get a bat autographed by Yaz and cross it with the other bat on the wall, and I mentioned it to Yaz about a week before the end of the season." This was the same 1978 season in which Bucky Dent defeated the Red Sox in a one-game playoff with a soul-destroying homer over the Green Monster. "Yaz made the final out, fouling out to third base," recalled O'Hara. "After the game, he went into the trainer's room and cried his eyes out. Naturally, all the media were waiting to interview Captain Carl. Finally, he came out and he kind of spread everybody out of the way and said, 'Dave, stay right there.' With that—his eyes were all red—he went to the bat room and got a brand new bat, came back and autographed it for me. In his darkest moment, he remembered me."

Is David "Papi" Ortiz actually the greatest clutch hitter in Red Sox history as current Red Sox ownership has officially decreed? Sometimes fans and media have short memories about such things, and past achievements are often diminished in the process. The other clutch hitter who immediately comes to mind when such things are discussed is Carl Yastrzemski, especially in 1967, the year of the Impossible Dream, when the Red Sox won the pennant against 100-1 odds. Yaz seemed to get a hit whenever the Red Sox needed one that year. It was almost supernatural—something out of *The Natural* or *Field of Dreams*. Yaz also won games with outstanding defensive plays in left field and daring base-running. In short, he did it all. As for hitting in the clutch, Yaz batted a robust .417 after September 1 that year (40-for-96), and added 9 homers and 26 RBIs. In the final two games of the season, with the pennant on the line, he went 7-for-8. And then came the World Series against the St. Louis Cardinals. Many hitters have tremendous regular seasons only to fade in the spotlight of the fall classic. It happened to Ted Williams. It happened to Stan Musial. How about Yaz?

In the 14 World Series games in which Yaz appeared (seven games each in 1967 and 1975), he batted a lusty .352 with 3 homers and 9 RBIs. His other postseason stats are equally impressive. In three games in the

1975 ALCS against the Oakland A's, he batted .455 and added 1 homer and 2 RBIs.

Yaz won the MVP in 1967 for a season that will go down in history as one of the most unlikely ever recorded. "For that one year he was Babe Ruth, Ty Cobb, and Honus Wagner all rolled into one," said Ted Williams. "He did everything for the Red Sox that year; if they needed a clutch hit or a stolen base, he got it. If the situation called for a ninth-inning home run, he hit it; if they needed a great game-saving catch, he made it."

When Yaz retired in 1983, he had become one of the most beloved players in Red Sox history and owned a long list of club records. The man with the once unpronounceable name was a household word in New England and throughout baseball. He is a member of the very exclusive 400-homer, 3,000-hit fraternity. He made himself a great ballplayer and kept in trim shape up until his retirement.

The 1967 Impossible Dream

The 1967 season was unlike any in Red Sox history. In fact, such a fairy-tale, worst-to-first scenario is a rarity in any pro sport. On opening day, the Red Sox were 100-1 underdogs in a 20-team league. They had not won a pennant in 21 years and had been in the cellar so long they were beginning to develop mold. Tom Yawkey had been spending money and acquiring good young players like Tony Conigliaro and Rico Petrocelli to join the veteran Carl Yastrzemski. He also had a new manager and a new managerial style. No longer was the Red Sox clubhouse to be compared to a country club. Dick Williams was a hard-nosed, no-nonsense manager who couldn't have cared less about pampering his athletes.

This was the year of the Yaz. Carl Yastrzemski's season was almost supernatural in its perfection. Day after day, game after game, he seemed to come through in the clutch and deliver yet another victory for the 100-1 underdogs.

The season came down to the last day with the Red Sox and Minnesota Twins knotted with identical records of 91–70, and Detroit one-half game back at 90–70. When the dust had settled on the day, the Red Sox were American League champions.

The World Series against the National League champion St. Louis Cardinals turned out to be almost anticlimactic. Perhaps the Red Sox were so overwhelmed by the pennant race that they didn't have quite enough gas left in the tank. They ended up losing in seven games despite Yaz continuing to play like a man possessed, clubbing three homers and batting an even .400.

Despite the narrow loss, 1967 was an unqualified success. The years in the baseball wilderness were over for the Boston Red Sox. There would still be mediocre seasons to come, but the Red Sox had turned a huge corner and established a foundation upon which to build.

TRIVIA

What vegetable name did George "Boomer" Scott give to home runs?

Answers to the trivia questions are on pages 175–176.

Carl Yastrzemski, here in a 1963 game against the Indians, replaced Ted Williams in left field and, over a 23-year career, hit almost as well as the Splendid Splinter. The zenith of his career was 1967, when he became the last man to win the Triple Crown.

Luis Tiant:
Mound Maestro

"Loo-ie! Loo-ie! Loo-ie!" It was a thunderous chant that expressed a city's love for an extraordinary athlete and competitor. It echoed throughout Fenway Park and across New England and warmed the hearts of even the most cynical writers and athletes. Luis Tiant was possibly the most colorful and entertaining player to ever wear the Red Sox colors. In fact, he was one of the most beloved athletes to ever play any team sport in the city of Boston. The cigar-chomping Cuban pitched for the Red Sox for nine years and became the most popular member of the team. Watching Tiant pitch was one of the great joys of baseball in the 1970s in Boston. A Tiant start was an event, a happening, a magical performance of prestidigitation by a spellbinding entertainer. He was known as "El Tiante," and he won 20 games for the Sox three times, 122 in total. In 1972 he bamboozled AL hitters to the tune of a 1.91 ERA and a 15–6 record to capture the Comeback Player of the Year Award. In 1975 he helped lead the Sox to the pennant with 18 wins. He also defeated the Cincinnati Reds twice in the World Series, including 6–0 in the Series opener.

They sometimes called him "El Tiante Elegante," and with good reason—because while his physique may not have been classic, except in a mildly Rubenesque sense, his movements on the mound were poetry in motion. His arsenal had hardened baseball writers suddenly using terms usually associated with other sports, or even art forms—words like "pirouette," "gyration," "twirl," and "spin." His deliveries were almost worthy of judges holding up scorecards, each one a "10" (except, perhaps, the French judge). He reminded one writer of the old Bugs Bunny cartoon in which an orchestra conductor tries to conduct while a bee buzzes around his head. He swats and jerks and gesticulates, but the music that comes out is beautiful to behold. Peter Gammons put a

TOP TEN

Clutch Pitchers in Red Sox History

1. Dick Radatz
2. Jim Lonborg
3. Pedro Martinez
4. Roger Clemens
5. Luis Tiant
6. Curt Schilling
7. Smoky Joe Wood
8. Cy Young
9. Dutch Leonard
10. Tim Wakefield

numerical spin on his medley of moves: "Eleven head bobs, five bows, two cha-chas, and an olé."

"Luis doesn't have a pitcher's body," Bill Lee once said. "He's like Pete Rose in that respect; he makes the best of limited tools." Lee who had the fundamentals of pitching a baseball pounded into him by Rod Dedeaux at USC, went on to say, "I look at the way Luis winds up and goes through all of those gyrations and sometimes it hurts me to watch him throw. But I'm always amazed by his concentration and desire. He gives everything he's got to winning." He was the heart and soul of the Boston Red Sox, and there has *never* been a player to match his flair or pitching smarts, not Cy or Roger or Pedro, or Curt, or anybody.

Luke Salisbury, in his book *The Answer Is Baseball*, described Luis Tiant's delivery as a "turn-your-fanny-to-the-hitter, nod-at-the-center-field-camera, spider-on-the-banana-boat curve that could snap a hitter's jockstrap as it broke over the plate." Salisbury concluded his description with the following: "Tiant ought to be in the Hall of Fame."

Tiant's Hall of Fame credentials are impressive. His career numbers place him in company with many pitchers who are already enshrined. He struck out 2,416, had 49 shutouts—leading the American League three times in that category—twice posted the league's lowest ERA, and pitched 187 complete games. He was a 20-game winner four times and had a .571 winning percentage on the basis of a 229–172 record.

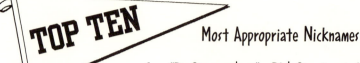

TOP TEN — Most Appropriate Nicknames

1. "Dr. Strangeglove"—Dick Stuart, notoriously bad fielding first baseman
2. "The Monster"—Dick Radatz, towering relief pitcher
3. "Way Back"—John Wasdin, reliever famous for the long home runs he gave up
4. "Spaceman"—Bill Lee, southpaw pitcher with a different take on life
5. "The Boston Strongman"—Jim Rice, who could check his swing and snap a bat
6. "Tomato Can"—Jack Lamabe, due to his ruddy complexion
7. "El Tiante Elegante"—Luis Tiant, pitcher/choreographer extraordinaire
8. "Chicken Man"—Wade Boggs; he liked chicken
9. "The Grey Eagle"—Tris Speaker; due to his premature graying hair and dignified carriage
10. "Caveman"—Johnny Damon; he looks like he just emerged from a cave, not a dugout *t*
    "Splendid Splinter"—Ted Williams, skinny batting hero *t*

His lifetime ERA was a solid 3.30. All of these accomplishments place him in the same category as Hall of Famers Catfish Hunter (224–166; 3.26 ERA), Don Drysdale (209–166: 2.95 ERA), and Ferguson Jenkins (284–226; 3.34 ERA), to name just three. If he is not a legitimate candidate for the Hall of Fame, then who is?

Keith Olbermann, in the book *The Big Show*, says this of Tiant and his Hall of Fame credentials: "Luis Tiant is Catfish Hunter with poorer marketing." Olbermann goes on to make a direct comparison between the two pitchers, one in the hall and one outside looking in. He points out that Catfish started 476 games, Luis, 484. Their won-loss records and lifetime ERAs are nearly identical. Tiant had more strikeouts than Hunter by a margin of 2,416 to 2,012. Tiant won 20 or more on four occasions, Hunter five. "Catfish's teams did better," said Olbermann. "Three straight World Series with the A's, two more with the Yankees."

One of Luis' countless pitching variations—incorporated while he was still with the Cleveland Indians—was what he called the "jaw-breaker." "Why the jaw-breaker?" he was asked by reporters. Without bothering to remove the cigar from his mouth, he replied: "My head stops seven times. Once it looks up; once it looks down; once it points the jaw at second base; once it points it to third; once it points it at the scoreboard; once it points it behind my back; and then before I let go of the ball, it points the jaw upstairs to where [Cleveland general manager] Gabe Paul is sitting."

In the 1975 World Series against the Cincinnati Reds, Tiant started Game 1 and shut the powerful Red Machine down completely with a 6–0 shutout. In Game 4 he threw an incredible 172 pitches—the equivalent of two quality starts for some of today's pampered pitchers—and gutted out a 5–4 complete game victory.

When Tiant pitched for Cleveland, umpire Hank Soar once had to field complaints—ironically from Red Sox hitters—that the pitcher's delivery was illegal. "He's walking a fine line of a delayed delivery," admitted the ump to reporters. "He can come down with his lead foot and delay his arm motion as long as he wants, just so he continues in motion without stopping. It's a very tough pitch, and it's amazing how he can do it just inside the rules and still control it. He's the trickiest pitcher in the league. I can't believe how many pitches and deliveries he's got. He's the only guy I know who can throw sidearm, crossfire from the stretch, while stepping in the opposite direction." Soar summed it all up with a comparison that anyone can appreciate: "It's a bit like rubbing your stomach while patting your head with the other hand," he said.

Hitter Reggie Smith, then playing for the Red Sox, once did a pretty fair imitation of a Tiant delivery. Leigh Montville, writing for the *Boston Globe*, was there to witness it: "[Smith] was working from the stretch position. He was holding an imaginary runner on an imaginary first base, and then he went into his motion. His leg went up, his head bobbed and turned like it was on one of those bobble-headed dolls. His body teetered and tottered and he almost lost his balance. Then he threw, whipping an imaginary fastball from behind his back." Montville concluded with some satisfaction, *"And that is what I'm waiting for. That's the only damned pitch I've ever seen Luis Tiant throw."*

Luis Tiant was the ace of the Red Sox staff in the '70s, winning more than 20 games three times and leading the American League in ERA once. He also pitched brilliantly in many big games, such as this one against the Blue Jays on the final day of the 1978 season, a two-hit shutout that forced a playoff against the Yankees.

Boston coach Babe Herman once likened Tiant's motion to that of the great Satchel Paige. "It's just like Satchel Paige's old hesitation pitch," he said. Mel Parnell recalled another ballplayer whose style was reminiscent of Tiant's. "He had a delivery like old Fat Freddie Fitzsimmons," said the former Boston ace. "Both had that spinning kind of delivery."

With tongue firmly planted in his cheek, former Boston pitching coach Lee Stange claimed that Luis Tiant had an unfair advantage while on the mound. "What people couldn't see were the strands of beads and the special loin cloth that he wrapped around his waist, under his uniform, to ward off evil."

Yankees catcher Thurman Munson was one of many hitters who were bamboozled by the pitches of Luis Tiant. "I think he's added three new pitches," said Munson in 1975. "Now he's got 50."

Carl Yastrzemski was arguably second only to Ted Williams as the most dominating and popular player in Red Sox history, but when Luis-mania hit Boston, Yaz looked around Fenway Park and declared: "This is Luis' place. He owns it and he deserves it. I think he's the most exciting athlete in baseball."

During the 1972 pennant race, writer Larry Claflin described the scene when Luis entered a game at Fenway Park against the Baltimore Orioles:

"The noise started in center field. Then it quickly spread along the right-field line. At first, we in the press box didn't realize what it was all about. Then we understood. They were cheering Tiant. As Tiant strode across the field, the noise grew and grew. The 28,777 fans stood and cheered his every step." As the game progressed and Tiant sent Oriole hitter after Oriole hitter back to the dugout empty-handed, the crowd was completely captivated. "They even roared with approval one time when he reached down to pick up the rosin," said *Globe* writer Neil Singelais.

Bill "Spaceman" Lee: Rebel Without a Pause

Bill Lee was a rebel when he played for the Boston Red Sox and he is still a rebel today. As a major league ballplayer, William Francis Lee was as out of context as Condoleeza Rice in a mud-wrestling competition, Dennis Miller at a Three Stooges film festival, or Tom Cruise keynoting an American Psychiatric Association convention. He was too smart for the room, too irreverent for the establishment, too hip for the jockocracy. He would have been more at home at a Warren Zevon concert or a Greenpeace convention.

Lee was one of those rare ballplayers whose off-field persona overshadowed his significant on-field performance. In baseball parlance, Lee is known as a "flake," a term that includes anyone who doesn't give pat answers to pat questions or dares to admit to reading a book without pictures. He was an original in a sport that often frowns on any show of originality. In fairness, Lee would have been an eccentric in almost any field he chose to pursue; but in baseball, he was considered positively certifiable. His often-outrageous statements and bizarre actions marked him as an oddity and ensured him a lasting reputation in the buttoned-down baseball world. They also earned him the nickname "Spaceman," a title he never fully embraced, arguing that his first priority was always Mother Earth. Nevertheless, Lee's record speaks for itself and places him in the company of some of the best pitchers in Red Sox history.

Lee's arrival in Boston was well timed. He arrived when social issues were front-page news across America and were especially controversial in this complex city.

Lee-isms

- "Pitching was 90 percent of the game, and pitching is what got him out 80 percent of the time." —On why Don Zimmer hated pitchers

- "Billy Martin was a dirty rat, so calling Zimmer a gerbil was not all that bad." —On his nickname for Manager Don Zimmer

- "If a guy spends all that time thinking about corking a bat, it's time that keeps him out of a bar. Gaylord Perry cheated his whole career, and he's enshrined." —On cheating in baseball

- "The strike zone fluctuates and you live within it. You have to have a good rapport with the umpires. Never allow the umpire to influence the outcome of the game." —On umpires

- "If you had had a dominant left eye, you'd be a lousy .200 hitter." —To Ted Williams

- "I used to beat them like they were a red-headed stepchild." —On his success against the Yankees

Like any respectable kingdom, Red Sox Nation had to have a court jester, and Bill Lee decided to fill the role. In fact, the Red Sox had jester, philosopher, and knight-errant all rolled into one 6'1", 210-pound package of left-handedness called Bill "Spaceman" Lee. For 10 seasons, Lee was the voice—some would say the conscience—of the Boston Red Sox. The southpaw sage was politically incorrect before politically incorrect became politically correct. He tilted at windmills, outraged the Boston establishment, and generally made life in Beantown much more interesting.

In Boston, a city where blue collar and scholar coexist, a city of stark contrasts, it is not surprising that he would be embraced by some and derided by others. When he all but called the city racist due to popular opposition to forced busing of black students to white schools, he alienated a conservative element in the city. But he won hardcore baseball fans over with his solid work ethic while on the mound. Fans soon

TOP TEN

Most Memorable Flakes

1. Bill Lee
2. Manny Ramirez
3. Mickey McDermott
4. Jimmy Piersall
5. Luis Tiant
6. Dick Stuart
7. Bernie Carbo
8. Sammy White
9. Sparky Lyle
10. Gene Conley *t*
    Pumpsie Green *t*
    Kevin Millar *t*
    Ellis Kinder *t*

learned that he was blue collar on the mound and applauded his work ethic and intense desire to win. Meanwhile, the collegiate community of Boston embraced Lee and related to his rebellious style. When Lee spoke out on social issues, the counterculture of the city lapped it up. More traditional baseball observers were less enthralled with the Californian rebel.

Bill Lee was born in Burbank, California, on December 28, 1946, the son of William Francis Lee Jr. and Paula Theresa (Hunt) Lee. His baseball lineage is impeccable. His father had played sandlot ball and later fast-pitch softball. His grandfather, William F. Lee Sr., was a highly touted infielder in the 1900s in Los Angeles. His aunt, Annabelle Lee ("The best athlete in our family," according to Bill) was a star in the All-American Girls Professional League for several teams in the 1940s and early 1950s.

Lee's own baseball apprenticeship took place at the University of Southern California, where he came under the tutelage of highly respected coach Rod Dedeaux. As a member of the USC Trojans, he helped to capture the 1968 College World Series.

Lee graduated from USC with a BA in geography, both appropriate and useful in that he has become a roving ambassador for baseball throughout the world.

During his big league career, Lee was a southpaw pitcher who relied on curves, sliders, finesse, and guile rather than an overpowering fastball to win games. He called the fastball a "bully" pitch and preferred to out-think his opponents. Teammate Dennis Eckersley once claimed that he threw "steak" while Lee threw "salad."

When Lee first came to Boston from California in 1969 and was given a tour of Fenway Park, he stared wide-eyed at the Green Monster and inquired, "Do they leave it there during the games?" It was at this point that sports journalists throughout New England gave silent thanks. He was immediately the darling of the dailies. They knew that regardless of the Red Sox's on-field prospects over the next few years, this refreshing newcomer would provide them with lots of colorful copy. Lee didn't disappoint. He was always good for an original quote, and not just some canned cliché.

He bragged about sprinkling marijuana on his organic buckwheat pancakes so that when he jogged to the ballpark he would be "impervious to bus fumes." He angered the California Angels by suggesting that they could conduct their batting practice in the lobby of the fanciest hotel in town "and never chip a chandelier."

When someone suggested that he should get a haircut, he responded, "I have a lot of theories and one of them is that my hair does not affect my pitching. If people are looking for nice, trim, all-American boys, why don't they go to Quantico? Because hair has nothing to do with baseball. Suppose we all took our clothes off and ran onto the field. It would still be guys like Pete Rose who stood out. Do you know what I mean?"

He saved most of his barbs for the Yankees, however, a team he had valid reason to dislike. He labeled the Yankees "Brownshirts" and "Nazis" and "thugs."

He didn't disappoint on the pitching mound, either, despite the fact he once claimed that the left field wall was so close that he "scraped his knuckles on it a couple of times" during his delivery. When he left Boston after 10 seasons, he had accumulated 94 wins, third most by a Red Sox southpaw, behind only Mel Parnell and Lefty Grove—this in a ballpark considered a graveyard for lefties. He ranks 13th overall in Sox pitching history. That's not bad when you consider the status of the guys ahead of him: guys like Cy Young, Roger Clemens, Pedro Martinez, Luis Tiant, and Smoky Joe Wood.

TOP TEN

Anatomical References by Bill Lee

1. "No, I've got about four valves and an aorta coming out and a superior vena cava and a lot of other things." —Asked by *Oui* magazine if, like Jimmy Carter, he had lust in his heart

2. "It's just the fact that they [women] have a lower center of gravity. They're built that way to protect their female organs for childbirth and then they spread out. You know, 'She was great till she was 23, then she started spreading out and couldn't turn the double-play anymore.'" —*Oui* magazine interview, 1978

3. "As the Red Sox continued to win, you could see the Yankee fans sort of shrivel up, like testicles in a cold Nova Scotia springtime." —On watching the 2004 ALCS at a bar in Hawaii with Red Sox and Yankees fans

4. "That's just an old Dewar's cap floating around." —After a doctor spotted a foreign object on an X-ray of his foot

5. "I've tried. The veins in his neck just get real big. I can see him on life support and some Red Sox fan runs in and says, 'The Spaceman is here to see you.' Instant straight line." —On trying to reconcile with former manager Don Zimmer

6. "Zimmer wouldn't know a good pitcher if he came up and bit him in the ass." —On Zimmer's handling of pitchers

7. "Hemorrhoids." —When asked what Zimmer would be remembered for, referring to his series of Preparation H commercials

8. "Anyone who would go out and sell hemorrhoid medication is asking for it. My advice to him would be to use bioflavones. I think we are interlinked, because ever since he's been doing those commercials, my ass has been itching." —Referring to Zimmer's Preparation H commercials

9. "He missed it by a couple inches. It should have been called *Asshole.*" —Commenting on the title of archenemy Graig Nettles' biography *Balls*

10. "You have two hemispheres in the brain, a left and a right side. The left side controls the right side of the body and the right side controls the left half. Therefore, left-handers are the only people in their right minds."

Lee's overall Major League win-loss record was 119–90, with a 3.62 ERA. His best season was 1975 when he went 17–9 and posted a 3.95 ERA in helping to lead the Bosox to the World Series. But using statistics alone to define Bill Lee would be a mistake, akin to judging J. D. Salinger on the number of books he wrote. He was greater than the sum of his statistical parts.

Lee demanded perfection from himself and from everyone around him; when either party fell short, there was trouble. While a member of the Red Sox, his relationship with management can only be described as tumultuous. A founding member of a Red Sox faction known as the Buffalo Heads, whose sole existence seemed to be based on making Sox manager Don Zimmer's life miserable, he famously referred to Zimmer as "the gerbil" and openly questioned many of the strategic moves made by the beleaguered manager. "Zimmer wouldn't know a good pitcher if he came up and bit him in the ass," suggested Lee.

In 1975 he started Game 7 of the World Series and gave up a prodigious home run to Tony Perez—that Lee claims today is "still rising"—on an ill-advised blooper pitch. He still recalls the sequence of events that led up to the pitch and the resultant homer. "We were leading 3–0 in Game 7 of the World Series. The Reds had a runner at first in the sixth inning. For some reason, [third-base coach] Zimmer waves Denny Doyle a few feet away from second base, making a double play impossible. Sure enough, then Johnny Bench hits the ball to Burleson at short and Doyle is out of position to make the pivot. The ball goes by Yastrzemski and Bench is safe at second. I lost it and threw the blooper. Two-run homer. Someone should have come out and calmed me down. No one did. The next inning I get a blister and walk the leadoff man and he scores the tying run. The rest is history, but it should never have reached that point." The Red Sox went on to lose the game and the World Series.

In July 1975 Bill Lee was incensed when some patrons of Fenway Park booed the slumping Carlton Fisk (the same Fisk who would become New England's hero a few short months later). "This town doesn't deserve us," said Lee. "After we win the World Series, I'm going to get the hell out of here and ride into the western sunset. The writers are lousy and so are many of the fans. The only man with any guts in this city is Judge Garrity [who ordered forced busing to desegregate Boston's public schools]."

On the eve of the seventh game of the 1975 World Series, vendors could be heard outside Fenway Park shouting: "Full moon tonight! Get your Spaceman T-shirts."

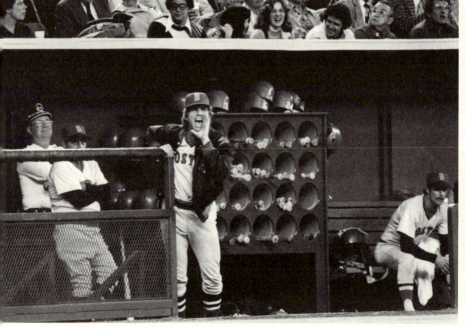

Unorthodox, brilliant, irreverent, flaky—whatever one considered Bill Lee, he was a darn good pitcher for the Red Sox in the '70s. Lee, here shouting out complaints to umpires during the 1975 World Series, won 17 games three times for the Red Sox and was named to the 1973 All-Star team.

On May 20, 1976, Lee was nursing a 1–0 lead over the Yankees at Yankee Stadium when Lou Piniella and Graig Nettles struck for back-to-back singles. Otto Velez then singled to right where Dwight Evans fielded the ball and eyed Piniella trying to score. Leapin' Lou was thrown out by a country mile. A mêlée ensued in which Lee was blindsided by Nettles and fell awkwardly on his shoulder. The Sox won in the 10th but at great cost to their playoff hopes. "We won the battle, but lost the war of 1976," says Lee. To this day, Lee is bitter about Nettles' perceived cheap shot. Recently, when he met the former Yankee at a baseball function, he says that the former All-Star third baseman didn't even bother to get out of his chair. "He hasn't aged at all well," commented Lee. "He looked like a duvet cover."

Lee was intensely loyal to his teammates and naïvely expected the same from management. When friends like Bernie Carbo (and later Rodney Scott with the Montreal Expos) were sold or traded, he took it personally and, on two famous occasions, conducted impromptu walk-outs, further alienating himself from the baseball establishment and narrowing his job prospects. Fined a day's pay of roughly $500 for the Carbo incident, he asked if they could make it $1,500. "I'd like to have the whole weekend," he explained.

Lee left Boston in a trade with the Montreal Expos for Stan Papi, an indignity that still rankles the proud competitor. When the trade was announced, he covered his disappointment with bravado, saying of the 1978 team that had lost the pennant in a one-game playoff to the Yankees, "Who wants to be with a team that will go down in history alongside the '64 Phillies and the '67 Arabs?"

But Lee's baseball legacy will always be that of flake. He will always be the guy who refused to conform. He will always be the "Spaceman."

Lee got considerable pleasure from the Red Sox victory in the 2004 World Series, and even more residual pleasure from the ALCS comeback over the hated Yankees. He later claimed that Steinbrenner was moving the Yankees to the Philippines where they would play under the new name "The Manila Folders."

Like Yogi Berra and Casey Stengel before him, many of Lee's comments have made their way into the baseball vernacular and ensured his reputation for eccentricity. When Sparky Anderson boasted before Game 7 of the 1975 World Series that regardless of the outcome, his pitcher Don Gullett was going to the Hall of Fame, Lee countered with, "Regardless of the outcome of this game, I'm going to the Eliot Lounge." If there were a hall of fame for originals, Lee would be enshrined immediately.

Lee left the majors for good in 1982 following arguments with Montreal management, and claims that he has been blackballed from major league baseball ever since. The years following Lee's departure from the majors can best be described as nomadic. At this writing, Lee still plays baseball and shows little sign of slowing down. Since leaving the major leagues, he has been an effective, if somewhat unorthodox, ambassador for the game in such places as Cuba, China, the former Soviet Union, and small-town Canada.

Lee and wife Diana live in Craftsbury, Vermont. The Spaceman has two sons (Michael and Andy) and two daughters (Caitlin and Anna) from previous marriages. Aside from his continuing baseball saga, Lee also owns The Old Bat Company, which specializes in maple, ash, and yellow birch bats "from old-growth forest."

Actor Woody Harrelson owns the movie rights to the Bill Lee story, and it will be interesting to see who is cast in the title role. He'll have to be equal parts showman and athlete. Baseball needs more guys like Bill Lee. Thank God he's trying to proselytize the entire world to his baseball religion.

Yaz's Teams

Frank Malzone

The Red Sox have had their share of fine third basemen through the years, guys like Jimmy Collins, Larry Gardner, Rico Petrocelli, Wade Boggs, Bill Mueller, and Carney Lansford, to name just a few. But the man who is most connected to the position in the minds of long-time fans is Frank Malzone. Malzone was born in the Bronx, just a deep-in-the-hole throw from Yankee Stadium.

In his first full season in the majors, 1957, Malzone batted .292 and added 103 RBIs. He also led all American League third sackers in games played, putouts, assists, double plays, errors, and fielding percentage—quite a debut for a newcomer. On September 24 of that year he tied the AL record for most assists in a single game with 10. He captured the first of three career Gold Gloves that year and went on to lead the league in DPs from 1957 to 1961.

Malzone appeared in seven All-Star Games and homered in the second of two All-Star Games held in 1959.

Dick Stuart: Dr. Strangeglove

Stuart was sometimes called "Dr. Strangeglove." Other times he was "Stonefingers" or "Cement Hands" or, ironically, "Old Golden Glove." Stuart was to defensive baseball what Paris Hilton is to quality TV. He once admitted, "I know I'm the world's worst fielder, but who gets paid for fielding? There isn't a great fielder in baseball getting the kind of dough I get paid for hitting."

He paraphrased Ted Williams' famous statement about wanting to walk down the street and have people say, "There goes the greatest hitter who ever lived." Stuart's version was: "I want to walk down the

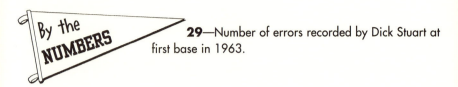

29—Number of errors recorded by Dick Stuart at first base in 1963.

street and hear them say, 'Jesus, there goes Dick Stuart.'" No doubt it happened frequently both during and after his colorful career, with certain less-than-flattering adjectives often preceding his name.

Stuart, like Michelangelo's *David*, had no use for a glove. To him, it was a Michael Jackson–style fashion accessory at best. In truth, his gamer probably still hasn't been broken in properly; the only balls that were housed in it belonged to the moths that inhabited the webbing.

Richard Lee Stuart was born on November 7, 1932, in San Francisco, California, and died in 2002 at the age of 70. The 6'4", 212-pound right-hander made his major league debut in 1958. In 10 big league seasons with Pittsburgh (1958–1962), Boston (1963–1964), Philadelphia (1965), New York Mets–L.A. Dodgers (1966), and California Angels (1969), he batted .264 with 228 homers and 743 RBIs. He was a holdout before he played a major league game.

He was swinging a bat in the on-deck circle for one of the most dramatic home runs in baseball history, when Bill Mazeroski won Game 7 of the 1960 World Series. Ironically, Maz was a perennial Gold Glove second baseman, a stark reminder that some players are one-dimensional, while others can do it all.

"I was kneeling in the on-deck circle, thinking I was going to be the hero," he told a reporter for AP years later. "And all of a sudden, I was out on the field jumping around."

As a member of the 1963 Red Sox, Stu clouted 42 home runs and topped the American League with 118 RBIs, becoming the first player to hit 30 homers and drive in at least 100 runs in both leagues. He admitted that singles filled him with "a sense of failure." He also set a record for most strikeouts in Red Sox history with 144. Stuart finished second to Harmon Killebrew in homers and promptly blamed the Red Sox pitching staff for giving up four homers in a September 21 double-header. He told waiting reporters who asked about the situation: "Don't ask me. Ask the pitchers. They threw up those fat pitches." Hardly the team chemistry that you see in Boston today. AL manager Ralph Houk once nixed him from the All-Star lineup because of a three-base error he had watched him perpetrate against the Yankees. Stuart promptly tore up a picture of Houk on his TV show.

It would be great subject matter for a doctoral research paper to discover how many runs he let in with his sloppy fielding, how much team morale was damaged by his attitude, and how many managers were given premature gray hair by his cavalier disposition. His ego was as inflated as his error totals. He arrived in Boston and was soon answering his phone, "This is the Boston Red Sox." As for his deficiencies at first, he allowed, "I'm no Hal Chase." He added, not surprisingly in error, "Anybody can field. Few guys can really hit a ball like me." He was also slow afoot, as Arnold Hano pointed out in a *Sport* magazine cover story in June 1964, "Stuart...would not beat Bob Hayes in the dash, or even Helen Hayes."

Similarly, he would not have beaten Henry Kissinger in diplomacy. He once asked the great George Sisler whether or not he'd gotten his Hall of Fame pin from a Wheaties box. He even had the nerve and effrontery to insult Ted Williams, somewhat like calling Paul Revere a Redcoat in New England circles. When the retired Splinter was helping out in spring training by batting balls to the regulars, he said in characteristic Ted fashion, "I am the greatest pepper hitter that ever lived." Stuart countered: "Of course you are, that's all you old guys can do." Ted countered by saying that he had just read an article in the newspaper about "the thing that you do best. Giving somebody the shaft." The "somebody" that Ted was referring to was his friend and former teammate Johnny Pesky. In an article in the *Arizona Republic*, Stuart had taken an indirect shot at his manager by suggesting that "the team always makes the manager." This is the same guy who once inspired teammate Dick Groat by telling him he'd be sure to hit .300. "You'll hit .150 the first half and .150 the second half."

Even before he arrived in the major leagues, Stuart was making headlines. As an outfielder for Lincoln of the Class A Western League, he stroked 66 homers and drove in 158 runs. Thereafter, he included the number "66" when he signed his autograph. Perhaps he should have added another "6" because he had a devil of a time in the field. In his first season in Pittsburgh, despite being moved to first base, he committed an astonishing 16 errors in 64 games. "Everybody liked Dick," said former Pirates teammate Dick Schofield, "but he did have trouble with that leather thing." That's like saying the *Titanic* had trouble with "that ice thing."

By the time he reached the Red Sox, his fielding had not improved, and he managed to misplay 29 balls in 1963. Ironically, he also led AL first basemen in both putouts and assists.

Stuart was the classic example of putting the worst fielder at first base. If the designated hitter rule had been in effect in his time, he would have been the prototype.

One of Stuart's faults was egomania. He was like poison on a ballclub and selfishly undermined the authority of management time and again. He was concerned only with his own offensive accomplishments and once admitted that he wore a uniform two sizes too small because "looking 'bitchin' adds 20 points to my average." Writer Larry Merchant once observes in *Sport* magazine, "At first base he resembled a dinosaur egg. Stuart's trouble…is that he hates all pitchers, including his own." A former manager conjectured that he might have misunderstood the pregame announcement about "not interfering with a ball in play." A minor league manager complained, "You're losing more games through the middle of your legs than you're winning with your bat."

In a case of the exception proving the rule, Stuart made a fine defensive play on July 3, 1964, with the California Angels leading 3–1 and one out in the eighth inning. The Angels had runners on first and second. Barry Latman attempted to lay down a bunt but instead popped the ball toward Stuart at first. Instead of settling for the easy out, Stuart let the ball drop, then threw it to Eddie Bressoud at second to force the runner. Bressoud quickly pivoted and threw to Frank Malzone to complete the nifty double play and stop the Angels rally. A heads-up play from a guy whose head was often up his posterior.

Infielder Gene Freese remembered a game in which Stuart had a bad day in the field—even by his rather low standards. Big Stu had managed to botch the first three ground balls that were hit to him. And then a strange thing happened. He made a spectacular play on the fourth, stabbing the liner with the grace of Hal Chase. However, as he motioned to the pitcher that he would make the play solo, he threw the ball away down the right-field line.

"We'd have had the guy at third," Freese admitted, "but I was laughing too hard."

Perhaps Bill James, the guru of statistics, inadvertently paid Dick Stuart the biggest compliment when he spoke of another notoriously bad fielder, Willie Aikens. "Makes Dick Stuart look like a gazelle," observed James in *The Baseball Abstract*. "Couldn't scoop out a low throw with a back hoe....If there is someone worse than Aikens, he must be playing with a machete." It is perhaps unkind to point out that Stuart did, in fact resemble a gazelle—with a glove on his hoof. But there was little point in tossing further backhand compliments Stuart's way. He probably would have missed them, anyway.

Dick Williams became the Red Sox manager at the start of the 1967 season. Not much was expected from Boston, which had finished ninth the year before, but Williams, here with the Cardinals' Roger Maris before Game 2 of the 1967 World Series, guided Boston to their first pennant in 21 years.

Dick Williams: Old School

In 1967 Dick Williams managed the Boston Red Sox to the American League pennant. He did it with a no-nonsense approach that treated all players equally and without favor. "Williams treats everyone the same," said first baseman George Scott, "like excrement." When he was asked if the Red Sox would have a team captain, he replied, "No team captains. I'm the only chief. The rest of them are Indians."

Even the stars did not escape Williams' biting humor. When Williams and Billy Herman were discussing Jackie Robinson one day, he turned to Yaz and said, "Carl, you run the bases just like Robinson did. The only difference is that you get caught."

Chuck Schilling

Chuck Schilling came up to the Boston Red Sox in 1961 along with Carl Yastrzemski. They became such great friends that Yaz is godfather to Schilling's daughter. The two infielders came up through the Red Sox minor league system as a highly touted double-play combo—Yaz at shortstop and Schilling at second. Yastrzemski soon moved from short to left field, where he had the daunting task of replacing Ted Williams. Schilling remained at second base for the Red Sox until 1965. Schilling was Yaz's roommate for five years and was witness to his baptism of fire in the major leagues. "Carl was under a great deal of pressure back then because he was replacing Ted Williams in left field," he told the *Boston Herald*'s Joe Gordon.

TRIVIA

Which Red Sox pitcher started, finished, and won both Games 1 and 4 of the 1975 World Series?

Answers to the trivia questions are on pages 175–176.

"He was a nervous type, just couldn't sit still for more than a couple of minutes, which was probably a result of that pressure....I think it ate away at him. He hit .260 [.266 to be exact] that first year, and it bothered him."

Schilling was involved in one of the most bizarre and exciting innings in Red Sox history. On Father's Day, June 18, 1961, the Red Sox were playing the Washington Senators in the first game of a double-header at Fenway Park. The Senators were leading the Sox 12–5 with two out in the bottom of the ninth—and the Red Sox won the game 13–12!

"When you think of it," said Schilling years later, "it was something. All I remember is that we kept going up there swinging, kept scoring, and kept going until we reached 13."

The Senators pitcher that day was rookie Carl Mathias, a southpaw who was looking for his first major league "W." It looked like a sure thing when he got dangerous Vic Wertz to ground out. Don Buddin then singled, but Mathias struck out Billy Harrell and was one out from victory. And then all hell broke loose: Schilling singled, putting runners on first and second. Carroll Hardy singled to score Buddin as Schilling went to third. It was now 12–6. Gary Geiger drew a walk to fill the bases, and Senators manager Mickey Vernon finally gave the hook to Mathias and replaced him with Dave Sisler. The reliever proceeded to walk Jackie Jensen and Frank Malzone to make the score 12–8. Catcher Jim Pagliaroni then stepped to the plate and hit a grand slam to tie the score at 12–12. Wertz then walked. Sisler was replaced by Marty Kutyna. Buddin singled to put runners on first and second. Red Sox manager Pinky Higgins put Pete Runnels in to run for Wertz. Russ Nixon pinch-hit for Harrell and hit a seeing-eye single past second baseman Chuck Cottier to complete one of the most unlikely comebacks in Red Sox—and major league—history.

Eddie Bressoud: The Other Streak

When people think of hitting streaks, they think of Joe DiMaggio, who hit in a major league–record 56 consecutive games, or his brother Dom DiMaggio, who holds the Red Sox record of hitting in straight games with 34. Eddie Bressoud's name seldom comes up in such conversations, but it should. Bressoud, who played for the Sox from 1962 to 1965, holds the mark for the longest Red Sox streak from the first day of the season. Eddie began his hit streak on Opening Day of 1964 at Yankee Stadium against formidable opposition. Pitcher Whitey Ford was on the way to a 17–6 record that season, but steady Eddie got three hits that day off the future Hall of Famer as the Red Sox beat the Yankees 4–3. He continued the streak for another 19 games before failing to get a hit against the Washington Senators on May 10. Always a team man first, Bressoud bunted to advance a runner to third in his second at-bat, sacrificing a chance to extend his streak.

Dick Radatz: The Monster

At first Dick Radatz did not care for the nickname "The Monster." Off the mound, he was anything but. He later embraced it and made it a part of his mystique. The idea of this 6'5", 260-pound behemoth striding to the mound was enough to make any hitter quake in his cleats. In the early '60s, a Boston newspaper sponsored a contest to come up with a new nickname for Radatz. The winning submission was "Smokey Dick." All of a sudden, "The Monster" didn't seem so bad.

From 1962 to 1966, Radatz's entry into a game was an event. When the score was close in late innings and the starter was in trouble, the call went out to the bullpen for "The Monster" to warm up. He jumped aboard the electric cart and headed toward the mound like General Patton in an army jeep. After several warm-up pitches—in full and awesome view of the opposing hitters—he settled in and threw nothing but fastballs. When the game was over and Radatz had saved or won the game, he lifted both arms in a victory salute as he left the mound to the cheers of Red Sox fans.

TRIVIA

Which Red Sox player captured both MVP and Rookie of the Year honors in 1975?

Answers to the trivia questions are on pages 175–176.

As a student at Michigan State on a baseball and basketball scholarship, the 6'5" Radatz also attracted the attention of football coach Biggie Munn. "You're Radatz, aren't you?" he asked one day. "How come you didn't come out for football?" Radatz may have been a monster, but he wanted no part of the gridiron. "No thanks, Mr. Munn," he replied. "I don't like raw meat."

Mike Andrews: Never the Twine Shall Meet

For the past 20 years, Mike Andrews has been best known as the articulate and effective chairman of the Jimmy Fund. His leadership has ensured that donations to support research into cancer in children will continue to grow.

Mike Andrews played a pretty fair second base for the Boston Red Sox from 1966 to 1970, but with a lifetime .258 batting average, he was always looking for an edge at the plate. One day he found a few strands of rope from the drag the ground crew used to smooth the base paths. He pocketed the strands and promptly went 2-for-4. The next game brought more batting success. On the third day, Andrews decided he was being silly and discarded the talisman. He went hitless. Naturally, he tried to find his good luck charm, but unfortunately, he had come to the end of his rope—literally. His string of hits was over. "I must have looked like a wacko digging around for rope strands," he told Dave Nightingale of *The Sporting News*. Unfortunately, the next season the Red Sox moved to a metal infield drag. "I had a season-long slump," claimed Andrews.

Sparky Lyle: Another One Who Got Away

Despite winning the World Series with the New York Yankees in 1978, former Red Sox reliever Sparky Lyle was less than gracious with the quality of the ring he received from owner George Steinbrenner: "I wanted to find out if the diamond was for real so I cut the glass on my coffee table with it. Then I found out the coffee table was worth more than the ring." Lyle cut his teeth as a rookie with Boston during their World Series run in 1967, which the Sox lost to the Cardinals, 4 games to 3. He shined in relief for the Red Sox through the 1971 season, but came to real fame as a member of the "Bronx Zoo"—the nickname he gave to the 1978 Yankees team in his book of the same name.

Luis Aparicio: Stylishly Stealing Home

Luis Aparicio was already well on his way to the Hall of Fame when he joined the Boston Red Sox from the Chicago White Sox in 1971. The treatment he received at the hands of Red Sox players, however, scarcely suggested that they stood in awe of the base-stealing pioneer. In 1973 Aparicio had received the okay from management to head home to Venezuela a few days early. "Little Louie" was known for his sartorial splendor and had shipped his vast wardrobe of designer suits, shirts, and trousers on ahead so that he could greet his adoring countrymen in style. He saved his best outfit for the flight home to Caracas. By now, Aparicio knew that there were forces of evil in the Red Sox dressing room just waiting to strike. He guarded his suit as if it were the crown jewels. After each at-bat, he returned to stand guard at his locker. Unfortunately, he didn't count on the deviousness of the Boston Slashers, as explained by Yaz himself in *The Sporting News*:

"When he had to leave to bat, either Doug [Griffin] or I, or one of the clubhouse kids went to work. We cut the legs of the pants one leg at a time and we taped them back together. Then we cut the coat in half and cut the sleeves off. Then we cut up the shirt and finally his shoes and we nailed the shoes to the floor. But we kept taping everything back together and hung them in his locker so it didn't look like anything was wrong. He didn't suspect anything."

Aparicio finished the game and thought he was home free. He soon found out otherwise, according to Yaz. "He took a quick shower and rushed around the clubhouse saying good-bye to everyone. Then he started getting dressed, and everything started falling apart. He had to borrow a T-shirt from one of the clubhouse kids and he wore that and a pair of shorts and sneakers home. He's a meticulous dresser and he had to go home like that."

Ken Harrelson: The Stylish Hawk

One of the coolest players to ever play baseball in Boston has to be Ken "Hawk" Harrelson, who played one full season for the Sox in 1968. Harrelson was the embodiment of the mod craze of the late 1960s. He went to a hair stylist and spent extended periods of time in hairnets under the dryer. "He's the only guy I ever saw who went in for a haircut and came out with more hair than when he went in," said a Boston writer.

He arrived at Fenway each day in a customized dune buggy painted lavender with flowers on the roof. "Lavender is my color, I guess," he told *The Sporting News* in 1969. "I wore a lavender suit to the baseball dinner in Los Angeles." When his agent arranged for him to appear in a Western movie with tough guy Lee Marvin, he quipped, "I suppose I'll be astride a lavender horse."

He wore black velvet pants, white shoes, and white sports jackets. He wore no socks. "He can walk around the hotel lobby in his underwear for all I care, as long as he hits," said his tough but pragmatic manager Dick Williams.

Rick Burleson: The Rooster

Rick Burleson was one of the most intense competitors in Red Sox history. He played for the Bosox from 1974 to 1980, and when he was

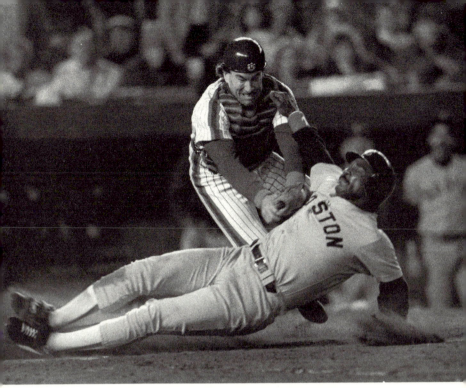

Jim Rice, here in action against the Mets in the 1986 World Series, helped turn around the fortunes of the Red Sox when he joined them for good in 1975. Over a 16-year career, all spent with Boston, Rice led the league in home runs three times and earned the American League MVP in 1978.

traded to California, the Boston media was extremely critical of the move. *Boston Globe* columnist Ernie Roberts wrote, "The fact that this is the year of the rooster on the Chinese calendar bodes ill for the Red Sox trade of Rick Burleson. Will the Rooster haunt them by having a bantam season?"

Jim Rice: The Boston Strongman

Jim Rice was known as "the Boston Strongman," although nicknames such as "Boston Bambino" and "Power Plant" were also trotted out on occasion during his long career with the Red Sox, which lasted from 1974 to 1989. "When Jim Rice hits a baseball, it's awesome, frightening," said Red Sox manager Don Zimmer in 1978. Rice was not an easy player for the Boston media. He was guarded, at best, and often downright rude in his treatment of the press.

Rice was an intimidating presence at the plate. In 1978 Kansas City pitcher Jim Colborn found out just how intimidating. After Rice had hit a massive foul-ball that just missed being a home run, Colborn hit Rice on the arm with the next pitch. Before proceeding to first base, Rice had a few words with the pitcher, and it looked as if the benches might clear. But after the brief exchange, Rice resumed his trek to first, apparently satisfied that his question had been addressed. "He just asked me if I meant to hit him," said Colburn after the game. Obviously, the answer was in the negative (what would you say to such a question from the strongest man in baseball?). "For a while, I thought I was going to be Rice-A-Roni," added the relieved pitcher. In Rice's next at-bat, he homered with a man on to help defeat the Royals 4–3.

When Don Zimmer was the third-base coach for the Red Sox, he had a chance to see Rice's strength up close. "We were in Detroit," Zim told *The Sporting News'* Bill Liston. "[The Tigers pitcher] had a 1-and-2 count on him and threw him a low, outside slider which was out of the strike zone. Jim went for it and got the bat as far as home plate when he saw it was a bad ball and held up on the swing. The bat snapped off about three inches up above his hands. He had the handle left in his hands and the barrel of the bat flew over in the Detroit dugout."

Butch Hobson

As a Red Sox third baseman, Butch Hobson was as tough as nails. And why not? He had once been a quarterback for Bear Bryant in Alabama, and Bear did not produce prima donnas. So when Butch took over as manager of the Boston Red Sox, everyone expected him to be a clone of his former football coach. Not so. When Hobson was being criticized by media and fans during the 1992 season, former Red Sox southpaw Bill Lee came to his defense: "It used to be 25 guys trying to please one man," said Lee. "Now it's one man trying to please 25 guys. I had a dream about Butch Hobson last night. He had a shadowy look to his face. An emaciated gray look to him. He's not what all you people perceived him to be. He's not a kick-butt guy with other people. He's a nice guy, a good friend."

Butch Hobson hit 30 homers for the Boston Red Sox in 1977, while batting ninth in the lineup!

Jerry Remy: The Rem Dawg Bites Back

Jerry Remy was not a superstar baseball player. In a career that stretched from 1975 to 1984, he hit a grand total of seven home runs to go along with a modest .275 batting average with the California Angels and Boston Red Sox. Remy was acquired by the Red Sox from the Angels for pitcher Don Aase and cash.

Remy set the Red Sox record for steals in a game when he pilfered four against the Angels on June 14, 1980.

When Red Sox pitcher Bronson Arroyo was promoting his new CD, *Covering the Bases*, in 2005, he made a trip to Maine for a noontime concert in Portland. A few thousand fans turned out to see him. *Morning Sentinel* Online writer Travis Lazarczyk allowed that the performance was "okay," but hinted that any Red Sox player would attract large crowds. "You get the feeling that one thousand people would cram into Monument Square to see Jerry Remy, the Nation's favorite color analyst, read the collected works of Dr. Seuss," he quipped. "Maybe ten thousand would come out to see Manny Ramirez do Shakespeare."

In a twenty-inning game against the Seattle Mariners on September 3, 1981, Remy had 6 hits in 10 at-bats. The feat tied him with Pete Runnels and Jimmy Piersall for the Red Sox record for most hits in one game. Nomar Garciaparra joined the exclusive club in 2003.

The native of Somerset, Massachusetts, is now approaching the level of stardom enjoyed by such Boston announcing legends as Ned Martin, Curt Gowdy, and Johnny Most. Certainly Remy is a celebrity who has reached cult-like status, as evidenced by the Rem Dawg signs throughout Fenway Park.

He could never be accused of hot-dogging it as a player, but when he's not busy doing Red Sox telecasts, Jerry Remy operates a very successful hot dog stand outside of Fenway Park.

Credit the sometimes acerbic but always entertaining Sean McDonough with bestowing the Rem Dawg label on Jerry Remy. The duo of McDonough and Remy had lots of bite, with the former Red Sox announcer often using the now sacrosanct Remy as his foil.

Jim Dwyer: Pig Pen

Jim Dwyer's nickname while with the Red Sox was "Pig Pen." You've got to love him for that alone. He was a down-and-dirty utility man with the Sox from 1979 to 1980, with the ability to help the team in a hundred different ways, all of them designed to get himself yelled at by his mother for ruining his best clothes.

Bobby Ojeda: To Bee or Not to Bee

Bobby Ojeda was stung twice in one game against the Minnesota Twins on May 22, 1983. Not only was he knocked from the game early, giving up five runs in one-third of an inning, his excuse was a real honey. He claimed that during the National Anthem, he was stung by a bee. His teammates were less than sympathetic. They wore plastic bags over their heads when he came in the clubhouse, made sure his locker was outfitted with cans of bug repellent, and mimicked a man being attacked by killer bees every time he approached.

Though he played for the Red Sox during the last three years of Yastrzemski's career, Ojeda left Boston for the New York Mets in 1986, where he posted an 18–5 record and started two games in the '86 World Series, including the fateful Game 6.

The Game 6:
October 22, 1975

If there is a single game that all Red Sox fans must know, it is this one. Game 6 of the 1975 World Series remains a watershed event in Red Sox history and represents the hope that springs eternal in the breast of all Sox fandom. It is our Iwo Jima, our Independence Day, our defining moment as a franchise. Even though we won the battle but lost the war, it represented a glorious historic achievement for the once-comatose franchise. The fact that the Red Sox went on to lose that World Series is important only in the historic sense. After Game 6 (a reference that every Red Sox fan knows: there is only once Game 6 for Red Sox fans, despite their having been on the other side of a markedly different "Game 6" in 1986), Red Sox fans were riding a high that for some of us has never ended. Game 6 was our epiphany. Our coming of age. Our coming-out party. Our Boston Tea Party. The Boston Red Sox had won the AL East title and then fought their way to victory against the AL West champion Oakland Athletics to clinch the pennant.

They were now battling the NL champion Cincinnati Reds in the World Series. The Red Sox were teetering on the brink of elimination, down 3 games to 2 to the vaunted Big Red Machine of Cincinnati.

The date was October 22, 1975. The place, Fenway Park. Catcher Carlton Fisk, the first unanimous selection for AL Rookie of the Year in 1972, came to the plate in the bottom of the twelfth inning, with the score knotted at 6–6. Just a little over four hours after the game began, at 12:33 AM, Fisk lined a 1-0 Pat Darcy sinker over the Green Monster, just inside the left-field foul pole, to win the game and force a seventh and deciding game. The game may not have been technically perfect, but it was superior to any promotional advertisement for the game of

Clutch Hitters in Red Sox History

1. David Ortiz—the plaque says so, therefore it must be true
2. Carl Yastrzemski—his feats in 1967 alone put him on this list
3. Wade Boggs—always setting the table for the big guys to provide the heroics
4. Fred Lynn—a true sense of the dramatic; loved the spotlight and always came through in front of a national showcase
5. Ted Williams—may seem an odd choice since he hit poorly in the '46 Series and in the '48 playoff game, but he came through in dramatic moments countless times, including All-Star Games, which were serious events, and not the mere exhibitions they have become today
6. Jimmie Foxx—a cold-blooded hitter
7. Carlton Fisk—Game 6, 1975 World Series; clutch hits don't get any bigger
8. Johnny Damon—came through time and again in the 2004 postseason
9. Manny Ramirez—hits the same in meaningless spring training games as in the ninth inning of the seventh game of the World Series
10. Nomar Garciaparra—during his early years in Boston, fans waited for him to come to bat in key situations

baseball that any ad executive could create in his most creative moment on the job.

"This is some kind of game, isn't it?" said hardscrabble Pete Rose, also known as Charlie Hustle, midway through the contest to equally unsentimental, hell-bent-for-leather opponent Carlton Fisk. And it was some kind of game. "I still say we won that Series," said Fisk, "three games to four."

Few moments in sports have eclipsed Carlton Fisk's Game 6, twelfth-inning home run against the Reds in the 1975 World Series. Fisk spent 11 seasons with the Red Sox, playing in six All-Star Games and winning one Gold Glove.

"Call it off," wrote columnist Ray Fitzgerald after the game. "Call the seventh game off. Let the World Series stand this way, three games for the Cincinnati Reds and three games for the Boston Red Sox."

Needless to say, Major League Baseball did not follow Fitzgerald's advice and call off Game 7. The Reds and Red Sox played, and the Reds won the World Series.

By the NUMBERS

6—Number of leaps made by Carlton Fisk before running out his foul-pole homer in Game 6 of the 1975 World Series.

TOP TEN

Dirty Sox: Dirt Dogs, Blue Collars, and Regular Guys

1. Trot Nixon
2. Butch Hobson
3. Jason Varitek
4. Carlton Fisk
5. Jerry Remy
6. Rick "Rooster" Burleson
7. Rough Carrigan
8. Bill Mueller
9. Carl Mays
10. Curt Schilling

1978 and Bucky "F*cking" Dent

The 1978 season was like some grand opera. It began with the Boston Red Sox on a record-setting tear. They were hitting on all cylinders and by late August had established a 7½-game lead over the Yankees in the AL East. Just when it looked like they would win the AL pennant in a cake walk, the Sox swooned and the Yankees surged. The culmination of the collapse came when the Yankees came to Boston for a four-game series with the Red Sox up by 4 games. What followed was a Red Sox fan's worst nightmare. Known in Boston darkly—and in New York jubilantly—as the Boston Massacre, the series saw the Yankees destroy the Red Sox physically, mentally, and emotionally. Each succeeding loss was like another nail in their coffin.

They lost the first one 15–3 with a piece of Yankees flotsam named Mike Torrez apparently believing he was throwing batting practice to his old teammates. Each member of the Yankees had a hit *by the fourth inning*. In the second game, they lost again, this time 13–2, as outfielder Dwight Evans left the game due to dizziness. Sox fans could relate to that condition. The next day's *Boston Globe* said it all: "If you need directions to home plate at Fenway Park, just stop and ask any New York Yankee." The third game featured Dennis Eckersley (who went 20–8 that year) on the mound for the Red Sox, while soon-to-be Cy Young–winner Ron Guidry (25–3) toed the rubber for the Yanks. What started out as a pitcher's duel ended up as another rout, this time 7–0, as the Yankees scored the touchdown and kicked the extra point with two outs in the fourth inning. The baseball world was watching with a combination of fascination and thinly veiled contempt at the Red Sox collapse. Tony Kubek, CBS announcer and former Yankee, said it best: "This is the first time I've seen a first-place team chasing a second-place team."

By the time the get-away game came along, expectations in Boston were low. Luis Tiant volunteered to try and stop the bleeding by pitching on three days' rest, but manager Don Zimmer ignored the pleas and started a rookie southpaw named Bobby Sprowl. Zimmer claimed he had "ice water in his veins." Whatever was coursing through his arteries, he was in the shower before the first inning was over. The Yankees went on to win 7–4, and the two teams were tied for first place.

The Red Sox continued to play as if in a daze well after the Yankees were gone, and it took a courageous season-ending eight-game winning streak for Boston to end the season deadlocked with the New Yorkers.

The one-game playoff—the second in Red Sox history and the second in American League history, the other ending in a loss to Cleveland in 1948—would be held at Fenway, and it looked as if momentum was now in the Red Sox favor. It was Torrez versus Guidry, and neither starter was brilliant on this day. Yaz homered to lead off the scoring, as the Fenway crowd went wild. The Red Sox made it 2–0 in the sixth, and only a supernatural play by Lou Piniella on a long Fred Lynn liner prevented a flood of runs.

With two out in the seventh, Bucky Dent came to the plate with two men on base. It has been said many times at many bars and even bar

Don Zimmer was named the Red Sox manager midway through the 1976 season, helping to lead Boston to 83 wins that season. The next three years he guided the Red Sox to 97, 99, and 91 wins, but it was never enough to win the division.

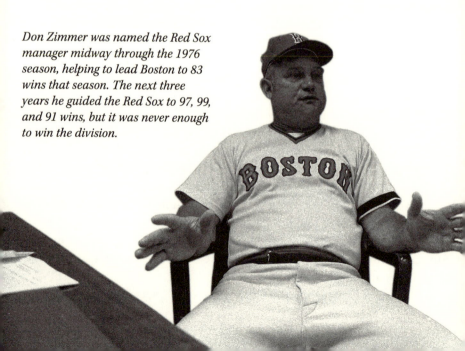

mitzvahs across New England, that Dent was only left in the game because it was a bit early to remove him for a pinch-hitter. When Dent fouled a pitch off his foot and danced around home plate in severe pain, the Red Sox faithful looked ahead to the next inning.

TRIVIA

Who holds the record for the most games played in a single season?

Answers to the trivia questions are on pages 175–176.

Mistake. His bat broken, Dent borrowed a replacement from Mickey Rivers and stepped back in the batter's box. The game was decided on a routine pop-fly. Only problem was, this particular routine pop-fly went over the Green Monster, making innocuous Yankees shortstop Bucky Dent (who had batted .243 on the season and half of that down the stretch) the most unlikely New York celebrity since Ed Sullivan. Other runs were scored in the game by both sides, and the final score was 5–4 for the Yankees, with Yaz popping up to end the Red Sox season. But there is no doubt in anyone's mind that this will—then, now, and forever—be the "Bucky 'F*cking' Dent Game."

Bill Buckner:
Goat or Scapegoat?

As a symbol, Bill Buckner is as essential to Red Sox history as Babe Ruth or Ted Williams. Anyone who doesn't know the significance of his name must have been living in Idaho for the past 20 years. Come to think of it, that's where Buckner ended up, so maybe his move makes sense. Buckner has become the whipping boy for every botched play, bad trade, managerial blunder, and egregious error in Red Sox history. He does not deserve it.

How would you like to be forever judged by a single mistake? Not a mistake that cost lives or even livelihoods. Not a mistake that was caused by a lack of hustle or showboating. Bill Buckner offers ample proof that life just ain't fair. In a career in which he: 1) won a batting title; 2) played in an All-Star Game; 3) achieved 2,715 hits, with 498 doubles and 174 homers; and 4) finished his career with a batting average of .289, Billy Buck is remembered for one miscue. A ball that he probably should have stopped got by him. Bad bounce? Maybe. The point is, that one play became a symbol of all that was wrong with the Boston Red Sox, and Buckner came to symbolize Red Sox ineptitude. Forget how many games the scrappy guy won for the Dodgers, Cubs, Red Sox, Angels, and Royals. Disregard his gutsy play while a member of the Red Sox from 1984 to 1987.

Bill Buckner came to the Bosox in 1984 in a trade with the Chicago Cubs for pitcher Dennis Eckersley. In both 1985 and 1986 he topped the 100 RBI mark while batting behind Wade Boggs, who invariably seemed to be on base. In 1986 Buckner batted .267, had 18 home runs, and drove in 102 runs. Buckner swooned in the postseason, however, batting .200 with only 4 RBIs and a single extra-base hit. Which leads to the following logical question: With the Red Sox nursing a two-run lead and up three games to two, why was a hobbled, slumping, aging—albeit valiant—first baseman still playing in the tenth inning of Game 6 of the World Series when a fresh defensive replacement was waiting only a few feet away in the Red Sox dugout in the person of Dave Stapleton? It's a question that no one seems able to answer.

Mookie Wilson's grounder skipped past Buckner, allowing Ray Knight to plate the winning run. The play demoralized the Red Sox and their fans, and they had no fight left in Game 7, blowing a three-run lead to lose the World Series to the Mets.

Red Sox first baseman Bill Buckner leaves the field after committing one of the game's most infamous errors, in Game 6 of the 1986 World Series against the Mets. A steady hitter, Buckner was also known, ironically, for his fine glove.

IF ONLY ... Dennis Eckersley had not been traded to the Chicago Cubs for Bill Buckner in 1984. Eck never saved a game as a member of the Boston Red Sox from 1978 to 1984. He was a starter in those days and posted an 84–70 record. After the trade, he went on to earn 386 saves with Oakland and St. Louis (he had three with Cleveland before coming to the Red Sox). Ironically, his last save (number 390) came as a member of the Boston Red Sox in 1998. He won four games and lost one that year. His final career record was 197–171, with a 3.50 ERA. Eck went on to the Hall of Fame. Bill Buckner went on to the hall of infamy after letting a seemingly harmless grounder elude him, opening the gates for the New York Mets to steal the 1986 World Series.

Fate placed Bill Buckner on first base in Game 6 of the 1986 World Series. Fate declared that a guy named Mookie Wilson would come to the plate with two out and two strikes and hit a little ground ball toward first base. Fate decided that Bill Buckner would be required to field this grounder in order for the Boston Red Sox to win their first World Series since 1918. Of course, rational people will correctly point out that even if Buckner had fielded the ball cleanly and made the out, it wouldn't have sealed a Red Sox victory, since the game was tied at the time. But rationality and Red Sox fandom are very distant relatives and seldom get together to ponder such fine points of logic. Seasoned in the Dodgers organization, where fundamentals are dispensed like mother's milk, Buckner was hobbled by persistent leg problems. The error was not his fault. He does not deserve the infamy that has been thrust upon him.

The ball went through Buckner's legs like a cold dagger through the hearts of Red Sox Nation. Fans forget that there were other miscues that led to this sad conclusion. There was plenty of blame to spread around, but it all got heaped on Buckner's plate as if he were some Bizarro-world Oliver Twist. Up 5–3 in the tenth inning, three outs away from the World Series title, pitcher Calvin Schiraldi took the mound and quickly disposed of Wally Backman and Keith Hernandez. Then Gary Carter singled up the middle. Pinch-hitter Kevin Mitchell singled to put runners on first and second. Ray Knight then hit an "excuse me" fly ball to center that fell in and plated Carter, making it 5–4 Boston. Mitchell took third base. Enter sinkerball specialist Bob Stanley, as a collective sweat broke out on Red Sox fans back in New England. Steamer Stanley quickly registered a strike on Mookie Wilson and then threw two balls. Wilson fouled off the next offering, and the Red Sox were one strike away from Nirvana. Two fouled-off pitches later the drama had built to unbearable levels. And then Stanley unleashed a sinker that eluded catcher Rich Gedman and rolled to the backstop. Mitchell scored, and Knight took third. The score was now 5–5. This was the preamble to Bill Buckner, the opening act to a tragedy, the main course before the sour dessert.

When you think of jolly old England, you usually think of Big Ben, Buckingham Palace, bobbies, bitter beer, and buses of the double-deck variety. So when Bill Buckner—then a hitting coach for the Toronto Blue Jays—visited London in 1993, he thought he would be mercifully anonymous. He was surprised to learn that his infamy had spread across the pond. "Yes, it kind of surprised me," he admitted to *Diehard* magazine. "They kind of joke about it. A couple of guys here, our drivers, they were looking at my legs and saying, 'You know, your legs aren't crooked.'" A headline in the *London Telegraph* announced: Billy Buck's Mission Recalls Memories of His Historic Failure.

Blimey!

Buckner lives in Idaho, where the only eyes to scrutinize him belong to potatoes and his cries of anguish fall on ears of corn. He deserves better.

By the NUMBERS

1—Number of bad hops the ball took before going through Bill Buckner's legs in Game 6 of the 1986 World Series.

21—Number of great seasons that Buckner played in the major leagues.

Wade Boggs:
Death, Taxes, and Base Hits

Wade Boggs was one of the most consistent hitters ever to play the game of baseball. He won a total of five batting championships and accumulated 200 or more hits in seven straight seasons. His trademark hit was the double, and he managed 40 or more of the two-baggers in eight seasons.

Why did the chicken cross the road? Perhaps to escape Wade Boggs. Boggs nickname was "Chicken Man" due to his insatiable appetite for that particular fowl. He consumed it before each and every game; his wife even wrote a cookbook titled *Fowl Tips*, featuring the bird in every dish. The habit began one year in spring training when he had chicken before an exhibition game and then went 5-for-5. He must be thankful it wasn't Brussels sprouts that triggered the success. Chicken to Boggs was like spinach to Popeye. He calls himself a "chickentarian."

Each chicken dish seems to produce different results. Lemon chicken equals 3-for-4, barbecued chicken may be a 2-for-4 meal, Italian chicken may result in a 4-for-4. But it's much more complex than that. (It would have to be, wouldn't it? Otherwise, we'd all be wolfing down Chicken McNuggets and playing third base for the Boston Red Sox.) Boggs explained his theory to sports columnist Michael Madden in 1986: "Say I have barbecued chicken again and I go 1-for-5, and then I have it again and I go 0-for-2 with three more walks, I'll know that the barbecued chicken turned out to be the walking chicken. Some chickens have hits in them and some don't." Boggs went on to say that 1983 was a "lemon chicken season," but when at midseason he was hitting a poultry, er, paltry .290 in 1984, his recipe for success had to be slightly adjusted. "I told my wife to go to the Italian chicken. Then things turned around for me." He ended that season with a .325 average, which is not chicken feed.

Whatever the culinary explanation might be, his batting eye was radar-like and his bat served as a launching device for stealth-missile–style hits.

Boggs played for the Red Sox for eleven seasons (1982–1992) before moving over to the Evil Empire in New York, where he earned his first World Series ring as a member of the 1996 Yankees. He finished his career in his home state of Florida with the Tampa Bay Devil Rays. As a member of the D-Rays, Boggs became the first player in major league history to make a home run his 3,000[th] career hit.

Base hits were as certain as death and taxes when Wade Boggs walked to the plate. Pitchers greeted him with about as much enthusiasm as Michael Moore was accorded at the Republican National Convention. Boggs was as predictable as a blizzard in Buffalo and as consistent as a metronome. In 1987 Boggs batted .363 to capture his third batting title and he followed it up with a fourth in 1988. He hit by the book, literally. To be exact, he hit by the book Ted Williams wrote on how to hit, *The Science of Hitting*. Boggs read it at least a dozen times and followed the batting commandments that Ted laid down. He learned the strike zone, he practiced constantly, he developed amazing hand-eye coordination, and he learned to be patient at the plate.

He was so superstitious (he prefers to call it "positive influences") that he would not vary from his pregame routine under any circumstance. He drew the Hebrew word "Chai" in the batter's box every time up. He took the same route to the ballpark every day, and once there, the same route to his position and back. He had a fixation on the number 7, entering the batting cage at 5:17 each day and running wind sprints at 7:17. A Toronto scoreboard operator once tried to alter his routine by having the SkyDome clock move from 7:16 to 7:18, but Boggs was not amused. He took the same number of practice grounders (150) every day.

When Boggs was dealt to the New York Yankees, his familiar No. 26 was already taken by Steve Farr. Boggs was forced to pick a new number—

but what number to choose? The superstitious batter pondered the matter for some time until a vision came to him. He was in a restaurant with his wife and heard the call of nature. It was during his trip to the men's room that he had the vision. For some reason the wallpaper in the john was decorated with the phrase "Pick 12, Pick 12." Boggs was so excited he invited his wife Debbie into alien territory to take a look. She

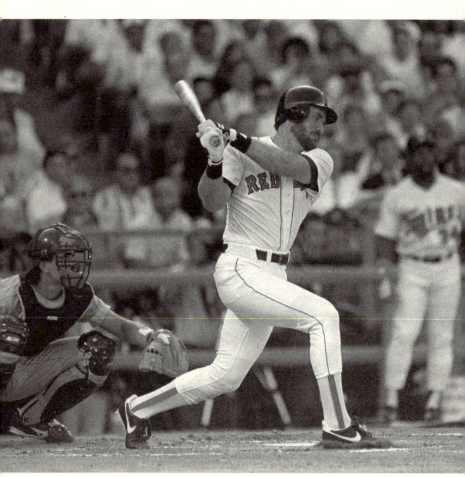

During an 11-year career with the Red Sox, third baseman Wade Boggs led the American League in hitting five times, played in eight All-Star Games, and won two Gold Gloves. Here Boggs goes deep in the 1989 All-Star Game, giving the American League back-to-back home runs after Kansas City's Bo Jackson had homered just before Boggs.

confirmed the miracle and, obviously, his new number on the Yankees was 12.

In 1985 Boggs batted .390 when he was 0–2 in the count—51.7 percent of his 240 hits came with two strikes on him. He batted .368 for the season, and an incredible .418 at Fenway Park. To put this in perspective, only Ted Williams with a .428 mark in 1941 (when he finished at .406 overall) ever had a better hitting year at Fenway Park. In reference to the Splendid Splinter's ability to wait for just the right pitch to hit, Johnny Pesky said of Boggs, "[He's got] a little bit of Ted Williams in him." Boggs saw it as good fundamental baseball. "I was the person who invented *Moneyball*," he told Marc Topkin of the *St. Petersburg Times*. "Now these guys make 15, 18, 20 million dollars a year for doing things that I did—lead off, get on base, and score runs."

Perhaps the most telling and truly amazing batting statistic about Boggs was his avoidance of pop-up outs. In 1985 he popped up to the infield *only five times in 653 at-bats.* In 1988 he popped up precisely *twice!*

Boggs was a true clutch hitter, batting a robust .344 with runners in scoring position, and a cold-blooded .363 with the bases jammed. Boggs was to the on-base percentage (OBP) what Nolan Ryan was to strikeouts. With 3,010 hits and 1,412 bases on balls, he was on so often that he was practically a base himself. His OBP while with the Red Sox was .431, behind only Ted Williams' other-worldly .482. Jimmie Foxx' career mark with Philadelphia, Boston, and Chicago was .428.

Concentration was the key to Boggs' hitting success. "One of the things I learned in life is that if you build a cocoon, no one can divert you from your goals," he once said. For him, spring training was literally a "concentration" camp—a camp in which you honed your concentration skills. "I don't play cards," he once said. "It's wasted concentration."

Boggs was a doubles hitter and a hitter for average. Despite efforts from everyone, including Ted Williams, to make him use his power stroke more often, he hit just 118 homers in 18 major league seasons. The exception came in 1987, when he hit 24 home runs while still managing to lead the league in hitting with a .363 average. He was asked to explain the sudden surge of power. He replied that it was "one of those El Niño years...all the wind blew out that year."

Boggs was kept in the minors longer than most young hitters due to a bad rap on his fielding. "I call it seasoning," he said mischievously on the eve of his induction into the Hall of Fame. "Five and a half seasons and hitting .300. Once I got to the big leagues, I was ready." In an interview with Marc Topkin just before his enshrinement, he was a little more blunt, and it was crow, not chicken, that was on the Chicken Man's mind this time.

"In the minor leagues, they said I was an inadequate third baseman," he said. "Then I didn't hit for power. I'll never play third base in the big leagues. I'll never stay in the big leagues. I'm washed up. All of these things you keep telling me, and I'm going to prove you wrong. Well July 31 [the Hall of Fame ceremonies] when I take that lid off, there's a lot of crow underneath for a lot of people to eat—all those skeptics and nonbelievers and critics."

In 1976, playing his first season for Elmira of the New York–Penn League, manager Dick Berardino saw no major-league future for Boggs. "I'm the man who said Wade Boggs would never play in the major leagues," he confessed recently. "Everything was pretty much average at the time," he told writer Marc Topkin. "Average speed, average power, average arm. I said he had a great work ethic and he would improve, especially as a hitter, but I only projected him for Triple A. Maybe a fringe major leaguer."

Finally, the Red Sox brass could no longer ignore his offensive talents and brought him up to Boston. Once there, he was immovable. He batted .349 in his rookie campaign and caused the Red Sox to trade away defending AL batting champ Carney Lansford. With the help and encouragement of coach and mentor Johnny Pesky, he eventually became a fine fielding third baseman, winning Gold Gloves at the position in 1994 and 1995. But it was his hitting that got him to the big leagues and kept him there for 18 years. He won five American League batting crowns, and led the AL in hits in 1985 with 240. He retired at the age of 41 with 3,010 hits and a .328 batting average. He was not willing to sacrifice average for home runs, a fact that used to irritate the great Ted Williams. "They say he hits some long home runs in batting practice," Williams said. "Well, the games are no different. When the situation demands it, why not swing for the fences?" He went on to say that Boggs was "capable of hitting 20 home runs a year." But that wasn't his game. Consistency was. Wade Boggs was one of the most consistent hitters ever to play the game of baseball. He won a total of five batting championships and was elected to the Hall of Fame in 2005.

TRIVIA

How old was Wade Boggs when he made his major league debut?

Answers to the trivia questions are on pages 175–176.

Boggs told Steve Buckley of the *Boston Herald* that he never misses an opportunity to chide Berardino about his woeful lack of assessment skills. "I'll say 'Wow, you're a great evaluator of talent, Dick,' and 'How many Hall of Famers [have] you managed?' and he says 'One.' And I say, 'Who might that be, the guy you wanted to send home in August? That's me, Dick.'" Such early criticisms might have discouraged many a young hopeful, but not Wade Boggs. Obviously, Boggs used the knocks and put-downs as incentive, what Buckley called "the empirical equivalent of a performance-enhancing drug."

Some of Wade's activities boggle the mind, to say the least. He once asserted that he had escaped a knife attack in Florida by willing himself invisible. As a pastime he has been known to mimic the various voices from *The Wizard of Oz*. He has a severe fear of flying. He has been on *Cheers* (where he was "pantsed" by the gang at the bar, led by Carla, of course) and *The Simpsons*, where he was recruited to play for Mr. Burns' Power Plant nine. He says that he was once run over by his wife in the driveway, but emerged unscathed, except for some tire tracks on his arm. He was the subject of an infamous palimony suit brought against him by his former mistress, Margo Adams. He subsequently claimed to be a sex addict. He appeared on a Barbara Walters special and was not asked what kind of tree he would be if he could be a tree. It was rumored but

TRIVIA

> **Wade Boggs was kept in the minor leagues for many years because of his poor defense. How many major league Gold Gloves did he eventually win?**

Answers to the trivia questions are on pages 175–176.

denied that he once drank 64 beers on a coast-to-coast flight. He once said, "If Wade Boggs batted behind Wade Boggs, Wade Boggs would drive in a hundred runs every year."

Boggs was elected to the Hall of Fame in 2005 with the third highest vote count since the Hall opened its doors. Boggs' induction speech at the Hall of Fame ceremonies included the following tearful and heartfelt tribute to his father Winfield "Winn" Boggs, not surprisingly a former military man: "Daddy, I wouldn't be up here without you, my mentor, my idol. Anyone can be a father, but it takes someone special to be a dad. That's why I call you Dad, because you are so special to me. You taught me the game, and you taught me how to play it right. Without you, I wouldn't be here. Thank you, Dad."

A Wade Boggs' at-bat resembled a military maneuver with its precision timing, discipline, and regimented routine, not to mention defensive swings to foul the ball off at will and "live to fight another day."

They put shifts on Ted Williams and other great pull hitters, but how do you shift a player like Wade Boggs, who sprays the ball to all fields with equal ease? Well, you use a "moving shift," of course. At least that's what the Minnesota Twins tried to do in an early season game in 1986. The Twins shortstop and second baseman were positioned behind second base and one or both were then were put in motion, as the pitch was being delivered to Boggs. The Twins were desperate enough to try anything after the Red Sox hitter, flirting with .400, had deposited hits to all fields. The strategy succeeded in distracting the usually unflappable Boggs, making it tough to pick up the pitches against the moving jerseys. The umpire of the day, Ken Kaiser, ruled the move illegal, and Boggs resumed his battering of the now shiftless Twins.

In 1986, of course, the Red Sox were one out from a World Series championship when the ball eluded first baseman Bill Buckner. Boggs recalled the nightmarish sequence of events in the tenth inning of Game 6 for the *Globe*'s Dan Shaughnessy.

"I remember it all," he began. "In the bottom of that inning, we got two outs real quick. I glanced over my left shoulder and saw 'CONGRATULATIONS, WORLD CHAMPION BOSTON RED SOX' on the scoreboard. Harry Wendelstedt was the third base umpire and he asked me to flip him my cap when we won. He said he collected them from World Series games. Then [Gary] Carter hit the bloop over short. Then [Kevin] Mitchell hit the jammer over second. Everything started. Then all of a sudden we're walking off the field, and I said, 'See you tomorrow night, Harry.'"

Wade's son, Brett, born a month after the 1986 Series, was named after his hero, George Brett. He is a promising young prospect at the University of Southern Florida.

Mo Vaughn:
The Hit Dog

For eight years, Mo Vaughn was as intimidating a presence as can be imagined for the Boston Red Sox. Picture equal parts Jim Rice and David Ortiz, with just a dollop of George Scott thrown in, and you have Mo Vaughn. The 6'1" 268-pound first baseman had a glare that could have been registered as a dangerous weapon.

A graduate of Seton Hall, the "Hit Dog" arrived in Boston in late June 1991, but it was his third season that marked his real arrival as an impact player. He batted .297 and hit 29 homers while driving in 101 runs. He followed that up with a .310 average, 26 home runs, and 82 RBIs in the strike-shortened '94 campaign. In '95 he just kept getting better, evolving into one of the most feared hitters in the game while posting 39 homers, a .300 average, and a league-best 126 RBIs. The numbers earned him MVP honors in the AL. Vaughn hit 230 homers as a member of the Red Sox and finished his injury-shortened career with 328.

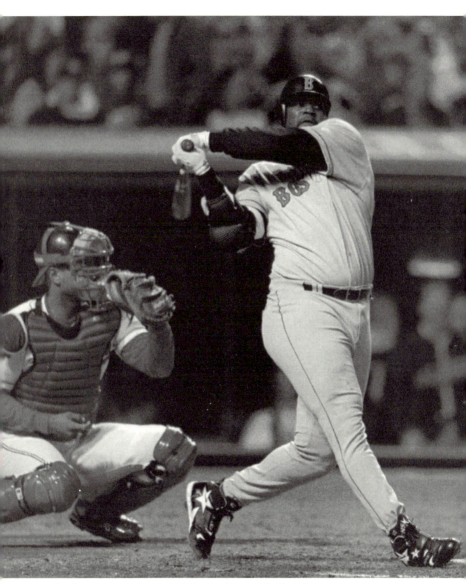

Mo Vaughn, here in 1995, provided the Red Sox with their first consistent power threat since Jim Rice. The first baseman hit 230 home runs as a Red Sox player and was named American League MVP in 1995.

TOP TEN

Stupid Statements by a Red Sox Player

1. "I wish he were still playing. I'd probably crack his head open to show him how valuable I was." —Roger Clemens, in reference to Hank Aaron's statement that pitchers shouldn't be eligible for the MVP award

2. "What can I say? I tip my hat and call the Yankees my daddy." —Pedro Martinez after a 6–4 loss to the Yankees in 2004

3. "Of course I heard it. And I'm not inviting them to my World Series celebration, either." —Reliever Keith Foulke, after a June 28, 2005, game in which he blew a save and a win in disastrous 12–8 loss in a game the Sox once led 8–5

4. "Dinosaurs didn't exist. The Bible never says anything about dinosaurs. You can't say there were dinosaurs when you never saw them. Someone actually saw Adam and Eve. No one ever saw Tyrannosaurus Rex." —Carl Everett, former Red Sox center fielder, since evolved into a member of the White Sox

5. "The faster you drive, the less time you spend with your foot on the gas." —Former Red Sox slugger Jose Canseco's paradoxical theory on fuel economy

6. "Dig him up. I'll drill him in the ass." —Pedro Martinez' fate-tempting reference to the Babe and the curse he wrought on Boston

7. "Ruth made a grave mistake when he gave up pitching. Working once a week, he might have lasted a long time and become a great star." —Former Red Sox player Tris Speaker on Ruth's conversion from pitcher to everyday player

8. "He's not as stupid as he plays." —Kevin Millar on teammate and friend Manny Ramirez

9. "Why don't you just point to where you want me to go?"—Dick Stuart to third base coach, after repeatedly missing base-running signs

10. "Now I know you're pulling my leg, because he was a left-handed pitcher. [Don] Zimmer would never let me hit against a left-hander with the bases loaded." —A confused Bernie Carbo, after hitting a grand slam against Seattle Mariners' southpaw Mike Kekich. He hadn't noticed the bases were loaded.

By the NUMBERS

8—number of Red Sox players left on the field when Manny Ramirez went through the Green Monster scoreboard for a pee break against the Yankees, July 17, 2005

40—number of strikeouts recorded by Roger Clemens against the Seattle Mariners and Detroit Tigers in two games

40–39—Roger Clemens combined record during his last four seasons in a Red Sox uniform (1993–1996), which is why it is hard to criticize Dan Duquette for believing that the Rocket was, indeed, "in the twilight of his career."

The New Millennium

The Yankees haven't won a World Series in this millennium (which started in 2001, of course), and the Red Sox have already won one, with 95 more years to go! Of course they started the last millennium well, too, winning five of the first 15. So let's not get overconfident.

Aaron "F*cking" Boone: New Millennium, Same Old Story

In February of 2002 an ownership consortium led by John Henry, Larry Lucchino, and Tom Werner took over the Red Sox reins. Larry Lucchino was made president of the organization. GM Dan Duquette, the source of much fan and player resentment, was dismissed, and eventually Theo Epstein, a 28-year-old Yale graduate was made the general manager. He was the youngest GM in the history of the majors. The new ownership made immediate strides, and for a while it looked like they might end the 85-year championship drought in their first try. In 2003 the Red Sox reached the postseason via the wild-card. After losing the first two games of the ALDS to the Oakland Athletics, they fought back and won the series, earning the right to face their oldest nemesis, the Yankees, in the ALCS. It was a tight series between the two bitter rivals, naturally coming down to a seventh and deciding game.

It was a classic even before the teams took the field: Pedro Martinez versus Roger Clemens at Yankee Stadium. For a while it looked like the game had been over-hyped by the media. The Red Sox had knocked Clemens out of the box by the end of the fourth inning, and Boston took what appeared to be a commanding 5–2 lead into the eighth inning behind the stellar pitching of ace Martinez. And then disaster struck.

IF ONLY . . . Grady Little had removed Pedro Martinez and inserted Alan Embree in relief in the eighth inning of the seventh game of the 2003 ALCS.

There is every reason to believe the Red Sox would have won the ALCS and gone on to win the World Series against the Florida Marlins. When Embree and then Timlin entered the game—after the Yankees had knotted the score off a drained Pedro—they held the Yankees scoreless for the eighth and ninth innings. In fact, the Red Sox bullpen had been stellar, indeed, almost perfect the last few weeks of the season.

Few if any fans expected to see Pedro take the mound in the eighth. He had thrown 115 pitches, and every Sox fan who had been paying attention all year knew that after 100 pitches he was an accident waiting to happen. It was clear to even the most casual of fans that he was a spent force; he had pitched his heart out and now it was time for a fresh arm to finish things off.

To everyone's surprise, Pedro emerged from the dugout and took his warm-up throws. It was a managerial decision that made Grady Little an instant part of the Red Sox lore of losing. Pedro coughed up three runs, and the game was tied. The Red Sox lost in the eleventh inning on a home run by an unlikely hero—the light-hitting third baseman Aaron Boone (remember Bucky Dent?) off Red Sox workhorse Tim Wakefield. The final score was 6–5. Once again, the Boston Red Sox had victory snatched rudely from their grasp. New ownership, same old Red Sox.

TRIVIA

Which former Red Sox shortstop is married to soccer star Mia Hamm?

Answers to the trivia questions are on pages 175–176.

A New Script:
World Champions

By the beginning of 2004, the Red Sox had a new manager in Terry Francona and a second pitching ace in Curt Schilling (newly acquired from Arizona) but were fighting the same old demons. By the July 31 deadline, the Sox had dealt Nomar Garciaparra, the most popular Red Sox player since Ted Williams, to the Chicago Cubs in a four-team deal that brought Orlando Cabrera and Doug Mientkiewicz to Boston. It was make-or-break time for Theo Epstein and the rest of the Red Sox brain trust.

The new-look Red Sox meshed both on the field and in the clubhouse, and the newcomers came through in style. The Red Sox finished just three games behind the Yankees and captured the American League wild-card. Riding the season momentum, they swept the California Angels in the ALDS and once again faced the New York Yankees for the American league pennant.

At first, it looked as if the ghosts from the previous year's collapse were still haunting the team. They lost Game 1. They lost Game 2. They lost Game 3—19–8! Fans were no longer praying for a World Series berth, they were pleading for respectability—just one win. *Please!* Finally in Game 4, at Fenway, good things began to happen. The Red Sox were on the precipice, down 4–3 in the ninth with Mariano Rivera on the mound for the Yankees. As straits go, they don't get much direr than that. Then pinch-runner Dave Roberts stole a base, and Bill Mueller singled the utility man home. Hardly earth-shaking, you say? The Sox then allowed David Ortiz to put them on his back, and he carried them to a come-from-behind, 6–4 win with a towering home run in the twelfth inning. Still no chance of winning the series, of course, but at least a measure of respectability. In Game 5 the Red Sox were again on the verge of defeat. The Yankees once again held the lead going into the eighth inning. Once again, the Red Sox got to Mariano Rivera and forced the game into extra innings. Behind the brilliant pitching of Tim Wakefield, the Red Sox survived a nerve-wracking top of the thirteenth and won the game in the bottom of the fourteenth on an Ortiz single. Things were becoming a bit more interesting, and hope that had been on life support was starting to revive, albeit slowly.

The Red Sox now had to leave the friendly confines of Fenway and enter the Evil Empire. Curt Schilling, who was bloodied but not bowed, pitched one of the most courageous games that have ever been recorded in major league history. He allowed only a single run, struck out four, and issued no bases on balls. Reliever Keith Foulke came on in the ninth to squelch a Yankees rally, and the Red Sox tied the ALCS at three games apiece.

In Game 7, the Red Sox had all the momentum. Johnny Damon hit a grand slam in the second inning and homered again later as the game was never in doubt. The Red Sox had achieved the impossible, writing one of the most incredible next-to-final chapters in the history of North American professional sports.

The final chapter would be the World Series, and the Red Sox had been this far four previous times since 1918, losing in seven games each time. Some skeptics in the media predicted over-confidence against a very good St. Louis

TRIVIA

Which of these past and current Red Sox players is *not* a switch hitter?

a) Reggie Smith

b) Johnny Damon

c) Bill Mueller

d) Jason Varitek

Answers to the trivia questions are on pages 175–176.

TRIVIA

Which future Red Sox shortstop made the final out for the St. Louis Cardinals in the 2004 World Series?

Answers to the trivia questions are on pages 175–176.

Cardinals team. But there was no need to worry. The Red Sox were not to be denied, sweeping the Cards in four straight to win the World Series and exorcise the ghost of the Bambino.

2005 and Beyond

The Red Sox of 2005 had a different look when they assembled in Fort Myers after a long winter of wining, dining, and TV appearances. Gone were Pedro Martinez, Derek Lowe, Orlando Cabrera, Dave Roberts, and Pokey Reese. Edgar Renteria took over shortstop, David Wells and Matt Clement were brought in to buoy the pitching staff. Perhaps the biggest off-season move was a non-move. The Red Sox succeeded in signing catcher Jason Varitek to a long-term contract.

In 2005 the Red Sox and Yankees were involved in one of the tightest and most exciting pennant races in recent memory. The seemingly scripted schedule had the two teams meeting in a season-ending three-game series at Fenway, with the Yankees leading the American League East by a single game. The Red Sox won the first game of the series to give them a tie for first place. The next day the Yankees won behind the stellar pitching of Randy Johnson and, because the Yankees had a better regular season record against the Red Sox, they were the AL East champs once again. The Red Sox rebounded to win the next day behind the pitching of Curt Schilling. The two teams finished the season with identical records. Even more incredible was this statistic: since the beginning of the 2003 season, including postseason play in 2003 and 2004, the two teams had faced each other 71 times. The Red Sox had won 36 of those contests and the Yankees 35. It doesn't get much closer than that.

The 2005 AL wild-card champion Red Sox had won the right to face the Chicago White Sox in the ALDS, while the Yankees traveled west to take on the L.A. Angels in Anaheim. The Red Sox 2005 season ended with a whimper and not a bang. In the battle of the Sox, the colorless variety beat the crimson 3–0 to win the ALDS and advance to the ALCS.

The Red Sox defeat was especially disappointing since it marked the end of an incredible three-year odyssey at

TRIVIA

Who hit the last
Red Sox inside-the-park
homer and when?

Answers to the trivia questions are on pages 175–176.

Fenway Park. A team with chemistry like this does not come along often and, when it does, it is magical. The Red Sox had captured lighting in a bottle, and now the future was uncertain. Kevin Millar, Manny Ramirez, David Ortiz, Bill Mueller, and Johnny Damon were names that Red Sox fans had become used to speaking and thinking of as a group. The idea that some of them would be wearing different uniforms next season was sobering for Boston fans. More disturbing still was the departure of GM Theo Epstein, the boy-genius architect of the Red Sox's first World Series team in 86 years and the visionary who was to lead the team for years to come. Nevertheless, the core the Red Sox remains intact.

The Red Sox of the new millennium are a diverse lot, reflective of a diverse cross-section of American society. The lineup features blacks, whites, Hispanics, free spirits, evangelicals, and born again rockers. Here then are your 21st century Boston Red Sox.

The New-Look, New-Millennium Sox

Bronson Arroyo: Music Man

Bronson Arroyo was named after tough guy actor Charles Bronson, and Arroyo is certainly a tough competitor on the pitching mound. But it's hard to imagine the star of *The Dirty Dozen* recording a music CD or wearing corn rows, for that matter. Bronson Arroyo's debut CD *Covering the Bases* (Asylum Records) includes such tunes as "Slide," "Down in the Hole," "Something's Always Wrong," "Best I've Ever Had," and, of course, one of the Red Sox theme songs, "Dirty Water."

Matt Clement: Quiet Quixote

The usually rambunctious Fenway crowd fell deathly quiet on July 26, 2005, as Red Sox pitcher Matt Clement was struck above the right ear by a line drive off the bat of Tampa Bay's Carl Crawford. Clement returned to pitch the remainder of the season.

Johnny Damon: Caveman

What can you say about a ballplayer who calls himself an idiot but has disciples instead of fans? Johnny Damon, the Jesus look-alike who has become among the best leading men and lead-off men in baseball, is one of the most popular Red Sox players since Nomar, Yaz, and Ted. Slightly blasphemous T-shirts at Fenway beseech WWJDD? (What would Johnny Damon do?) TV and radio commercials capitalizing on his flowing locks seem to be everywhere.

Boston is the kind of negative and cynical city where a man walking on water might be accused of not knowing how to swim. Although his quotations may fall somewhat short of the Savior, they are still enlightening, if not enlightened. "We try to eliminate the thinking," he once said,

Center fielder Johnny Damon triples in Game 4 of the 2004 World Series. Damon hit three home runs in the 2004 postseason.

and added, "If we use our brains, we're only hurting the team." When told of Alex Rodriguez' habit of rising at 6:00 AM to train, he offered, "There's been many a night where I haven't been to bed at six in the morning." Asked about being compared to God and his Son, Damon modestly deflected the compliment. "Those guys are awesome," he said as if talking about a couple of rival center fielders who were competing with him for All-Star selection. And then with just a hint of deity in his voice, he said of the 2004 World Series victory, "We shocked the world."

But perhaps Damon's most impressive and miraculous act was as prophet. At the news conference where he was introduced to the Boston media and Red Sox Nation, he declared, "When we win a World Series, we're going to be put on a pedestal and be immortalized forever."

So spaketh Johnny Damon. So it shall come to pass.

Johnny Damon may be the best leadoff hitter in baseball, partly because he uses his head. Never was this use of his noggin more obvious that during a bizarre series of miscues on a single play in a July 29, 2005, game at Fenway Park. Locked in a scoreless tie with the Minnesota Twins in the fifth inning at Fenway Park, the Red Sox were threatening. With two outs, Bill Mueller and Tony Graffanino came through with back-to-back base hits. Johnny Damon then blooped a broken-bat single to right, and Twins right fielder Jacque Jones threw home to try to prevent Mueller from scoring. The throw was off line and should have been intercepted by first baseman Justin Morneau. Instead, it skidded past catcher Joe Mauer all the way to the backstop, allowing Mueller to score. Graffanino, who had rounded third, also tried to score on the errant throw. Pitcher Carlos Silva, backing up the catcher, fielded the ball and threw wide of catcher Mauer, who had moved to cover the plate. Graffanino scored the second Red Sox run. First baseman Justin Morneau retrieved the ball and pegged it to third as Damon hit the sack with the intention of scoring. Third baseman Luis Rodriguez took the throw and quickly relayed it home to get Damon. The ball hit Johnny in the back of his head, and he scored the third run of the inning, thanks to a single and two errors. And somewhere the Three Stooges were smiling.

After the game Minnesota manager Ron Gardenhire summed up the events nicely. "Morneau should have cut it. Joe should have caught it. Silva should have ate it. Rodriguez shouldn't have hit the guy in the head." The Red Sox went on to win the game 8–5, thanks to a grand slam by John Olerud, but the fifth inning fiasco was what had the crowd buzzing on the way home.

In the third inning of a May 31, 2005, game at Fenway, Damon ran full throttle into the outfield wall in center field in pursuit of a fly ball off the bat of Jay Gibbons. After the collision, the center fielder's right eye was badly swollen, his cheek was an angry shade of red, and his right knee was badly bruised. "I'd say he lost the fight," concluded manager Terry Francona after the game. As for Damon, he said that he wasn't worried about a concussion. "I knew it would have been just a minor one," said the gritty Caveman. He left the game only reluctantly at the insistence of trainer Jim Rowe. "He's a tough kid," said manager Terry Francona. "I was not sure who he was talking to. He was looking at me, but I'm not sure he knew who I was."

His teammates were extremely sympathetic. The very next day a taped outline of Damon's body—reminiscent of the tactic used by police to indicate the position of the murdered body—was clearly visible at the exact spot where he had hit the wall.

"Dear The Red Sox,

I kind of promised this girl I would get her a sack of Johnny Damon's face hair. And, well, she's starting to wonder where that sack of face hair's at. I really like this girl (Suzanne, btw). Appreciate the help."—from an email to the Red Sox as reported in *Sports Illustrated*, July 11, 2005

"Bottom line," says Kevin Millar. "We've been cursed for 86 years. Mel Gibson makes *The Passion of the Christ* and he's taking all kinds of heat for it. Next thing you know Johnny comes in and looking like Jesus, and we break the curse."—*Sports Illustrated*, July 11, 2005, "Life of Reilly" column

"Sometimes they hit on me right in front of my wife. I mean, women are relentless, man, relentless." —Johnny Damon as reported in *Sports Illustrated*

"He throws like a girl." —Kevin Millar on Damon

On the field, Damon goes all out and never dogs it. Off the field, he has some canine proclivities. Johnny likes to keep in shape by running, and—wait for it—he sometimes runs after passing cars to add an extra competitive edge. "I think I can run about 25 miles per hour, top speed," he told *Sports Illustrated*. Sometimes I actually pass cars on Boylston [Street]. They realize they're in the company of either a great athlete, or a criminal running from something." And no, he doesn't stop at fire hydrants.

Damon is a child of nature and likes to roam around the clubhouse in the altogether, playing cards, doing pull-ups, and enjoying a pregame meal. "The guy is always naked," confirms Francona. "And then, 15 minutes later, I'll see him standing on second base."

Keith Foulke: Foulke Tales

It's an image that will forever be burned into the retinas of Red Sox fans: Jason Varitek jumping into Keith Foulke's arms after the last out of the 2004 World Series. Foulke would love to see a repeat of the world championship, but next time he'd like to alter the celebration just slightly. "Jason's catching me this year," he said midway through the 2005 season. "I'm not catching him this year. But that is my goal, to be in the same spot." In reference to the mini-dispute between Doug Mientkiewicz and the Red Sox over ownership of the 2004 game-ending baseball, he added, "I know my first baseman here will give the ball back."

Frustrated by his sub-par performance in 2005, Foulke was booed by a significant percentage of the Fenway faithful. His response to the booing produced a whopper of a reaction from the working people of New England. "They're not going to make it any harder than it is for me to go home and look in the mirror," said Foulke after a particularly bad outing. "Like I've told you guys plenty of times, I'm more embarrassed to walk into this locker room and look at the faces of my teammates than I am to walk out and see Johnny from Burger King booing me. I'm worried about these guys, not everybody else." As they say at BK, Keith, "Have it your way," but you can kiss your blue collar credentials good-bye. He finished off his mini-tirade with the words, "And I'm not inviting them to my World Series celebration, either." Is that the one across the street at McDonalds?

When Foulke was in rehab with the Single A Lowell Spinners and trying to earn a spot in the Red Sox relief corps, he was less than pleased with his early performances or the speed of his progress. After one particularly bad outing in which he gave up eight hits and four runs in 3⅔ innings, he was asked if there was anything positive to report. He replied, "Traffic wasn't that bad driving up, 40 minutes to get there. Wasn't bad at all."

And then there was the truck incident. Foulke speaks weekly with Michael Holley and Dale Arnold of radio station WEEI and is rewarded with a vehicle. He told a reporter for the *Hartford Courant*, "If you give me a free truck, I'll talk to you more." Perhaps Foulke needs to learn that if he continues to say stupid things, we will continue to not give a truck.

Terry Francona: Curse Breaker

Does your chewing gum lose its flavor on the bedpost overnight? How about the baseline? In an August 9, 2005, game against Texas at Fenway Park, Red Sox manager Terry Francona got into a heated argument with second base umpire Bill Miller. In fact, Francona was really chewing him out, when he paused to throw his wad of gum aside. Often such action will result in ejection, but not this time. It seems that Francona had just put the gum in his mouth and was inadvertently giving the ump a saliva shower, so he removed the offending chaw as a courtesy to Miller. "I should've gone back and got it because it was fully loaded and fresh," said Francona after the game.

Rich Garces: El Guapo

Rich Garces was a 255-pound (officially, he actually weighed more) relief pitcher for the Red Sox. His distinctive nickname "El Guapo" was given to Garces by a man who knows something about pitching, namely "Rocket" Roger Clemens. As soon as Clemens got a glance at the 230-pound Venezuelan hurler, he immediately dubbed him "El Guapo." Coming as it did from pitching royalty, the title was akin to knighthood, and it stuck. The literal translation may be translated "handsome man," according to Garces, but Clemens inspiration came from the movie *The Three Amigos*. The villain in that comedy was named El Guapo. "I'm proud of it," says Garces.

During his time with the Red Sox, from 1996 to 2002, Garces was a hero to many and certainly a villain to hitters around the league. In 1999 he was a key part of the Red Sox run for the wild-card berth. He went 2–0 during the stretch run and posted a 1.50 ERA. Overall he was 5–1 with a 1.55 ERA.

The Red Sox press box can be a bastion of cynicism, sarcasm...and truth. During a 2002 game with Garces on the mound in relief, an opposing batter bunted the ball toward the mound. Garces attempted to field it, but the overweight right-hander came up empty-handed. One unidentified beat writer was heard to quip, "If it had been a hamburger, he would have picked it up."

Gabe Kapler: Welcome Back, Welcome Back, Welcome Back

When most players win a World Series, they immediately say they're going to Disney World. Kapler said "Sayonara" and went to Japan instead. And if that choice seemed rather goofy for a world champion, you may be right. After leaving Boston for a $3 million contract with the Yomiuri Giants, he was back in the Red Sox fold by mid-summer 2005. Kapler was one of the more versatile members of the team, filling in at all outfield positions as needed. He had struggled against Japanese pitching ("The pitchers work slower and they have hitches in their deliveries," he explained to *Sports Illustrated.* "Here there's more of a rhythm") and was homesick for the famous camaraderie of the Red Sox clubhouse. Jason Varitek called Kapler's answering machine in Japan and played *Beer for My Horses*, a Toby Keith song that members of the Red Sox sang on plane trips in the 2004 season. "It literally had me in tears," Kapler confessed to the *Boston Globe.*

In an August 10, 2005, game against Texas at Fenway, Kapler appeared to have been robbed of a home run. The ball caromed off the lip of the Green Monster and bounced back onto the field. It was ruled a double. Francona and most of the partisan crowd thought it was a home run. The manager argued the point but eventually bowed to the inevitable and went back to the dugout. Trot Nixon, who was on the DL with a strained oblique muscle, had been watching the game on TV in the Red Sox clubhouse. He rushed to the field to plead the case for Kapler. He was promptly thrown out of a game he was never in. "That's my teammate out there," Nixon explained. "And he got a home run taken away from him."

Kapler's season came to an abrupt and painful end on September 2005 when he was rounding second base after a fifth-inning home run by Tony Graffanino. At first his teammates thought it was funny and were waiting to heckle the popular Red Sox utility man. But it was no laughing matter. He snapped his Achilles tendon and had to undergo surgery that put his future in some doubt. After a lengthy rehab of 12 to 18 months, he may be able to return for the 2007 season. The play was a baseball oddity. With Kapler disabled and unable to continue ("He wanted to finish it out," third base coach Dale Sveum said after the game, "the guy plays the game like a middle linebacker"), he was replaced by a pinch-runner who, several minutes later, completed his trek around the bases ahead of Graffanino.

Pedro Martinez: Ace

Torii Hunter is a now an All-Star but there was a time in 1999 when like all rookies he was struggling and over-matched. Facing Red Sox ace Pedro Martinez would confound even the most confident of hitters, but the fresh-faced Twins outfielder was no match for the best pitcher in the game when they first met on June 15 at Fenway. Pedro was cruising along with an 11–2 record (he would finish the season as the unanimous winner of the Cy Young Award with a 23–4 mark).

Pedro whiffed Hunter on three straight pitches his first time up. On his second at-bat against Martinez, Hunter was able to feebly foul off a couple of offerings. "It was unfair," Hunter told John Tomase in *Boston Baseball*. "I was like, 'What the hell is going on? He's coming at me three-quarters.' It looked like the ball was going to hit me. I'm diving out of there, and the next thing you know, it's nipping the outside corner." After another awkward foul, Martinez walked toward home to get a new ball. To Hunter's surprise, the pitcher offered some advice. "Stay in there," he said. "You're bailing out." Hunter didn't know what to think. "He was telling me how to hit. I was like, 'Okay. You're the boss.'"

If this were a scene from *The Natural* or *Field of Dreams*, the young player would have hit a homer on the next pitch, tipping his hat appreciatively to the veteran pitcher as he rounded third base. But this was reality. And this was Pedro. He promptly threw Hunter a change-up for strike three.

Pedro was the first pitcher in major league history to reach the 20-win plateau in less than 200 innings (20–4 in 199⅓, as a member of the 2002 Red Sox).

Traded to the Red Sox by the Expos at the start of the 1998 season, Pedro Martinez won 20 games twice, led the league in ERA four straight times, and won two Cy Young Awards.

Manager Terry Francona had to deal with a group of diverse personalities during the Red Sox march to the 2004 World Series victory. Pedro Martinez was one of them. Pedro often marched to his own tune and his own pace, as indicated by the following story related by Francona. "We had a workout," Francona recalled. "I don't remember now if it was during the playoffs or the World Series, and I'm the last guy to leave. It's around 5:30, and in walks Pedro. He's smiling, happy, and he says, 'Where is everybody?' I said, 'It was a 1:00 workout.' Petey says, 'I thought it was 4:00.' *It was 5:30!*"

Doug Mientkiewicz: Glove Man

No one can deny that first baseman Doug Mientkiewicz was an integral part of the Red Sox world championship season of 2004. The fielding wizard saved countless errant throws from short and third and prevented untold extra base hits with his wizardry at the initial sack. The deal for the Minnesota Twins' Gold Glover—part of a complex four-team trade that saw Nomar Garciaparra go to Chicago—happened to take place as the Twins were playing the Red Sox in Boston. "I was already dressed for BP and I was doing a press conference," he told *Sports Illustrated* in its August 1, 2005 issue. "Someone tapped me on the shoulder and told me I had been dealt." Mientkiewicz says that he didn't even have to walk across the Fenway turf to join his new team; he just cut behind the laundry room and "there was Pedro Martinez standing buck naked on my chair, saying, 'Welcome.'"

When a decision had to be made to trade either poor field–good hit Kevin Millar or good field–no hit Mientkiewicz, Red Sox Nation became polarized into two warring camps. Both players had many supporters, but ultimately Sox management decided to keep Millar, who for many symbolized the loose and irreverent spirit of the team, and send Doug to the New York Mets. Both players suffered through disastrous seasons in 2005.

Kevin Millar: Free Spirit

Kevin Millar's journey to Boston was as twisted as he is. He struck a deal with the Florida Marlins to offer him arbitration, and then place him on waivers so that Japan's Chunichi Dragons could sign him. To everyone's surprise—most notably Millar's—the Red Sox claimed him off waivers and prevented his move to the Dragons, to whom he was contractually committed. He therefore rejected the Red Sox claim. The Red Sox persisted. Millar finally fought his way through the three-way maze and emerged as a member of the Boston Red Sox, burning bridges with both the Marlins and the entire nation of Japan in the process.

Millar was a catalyst for the 2004 Boston Red Sox, keeping players loose and adding the active ingredient that made the clubhouse chemistry so potent. In August of 2003 he made his debut on Fenway's Diamond Vision screen as "Rally Karaoke Guy." The 30-second excerpt of less-than-high definition videotape was an unlikely motivator, but it seemed to work. Millar is seen lip-synching—complete with thrusting hips and swiveling pelvis—to Bruce Springsteen's "Born in the USA." The Red Sox went on a major winning streak after the video was first shown and, although Springsteen is still the Boss, Millar became at least Employee of the Month.

The video surfaced in late July of '03. The Red Sox were playing the Texas Rangers in Texas, and an old Lamar University teammate of Millar's delivered a copy to Red Sox officials. It is not known if the delivery was made in the dead of night in a brown paper bag, but Millar's friend is now an FBI agent. Red Sox manager Grady Little called the team together and told them that the FBI had been in touch on a matter of some urgency. He then played the videotape, and the Red Sox players were treated to a much younger Millar, with long blond surfer-style hair pumping his fist in the air as he belts out the song. The audience was appreciative, so much so that they decided it deserved a wider audience. Pitcher John Burkett took it to Dr. Charles Steinberg, who edited it before it was presented to the Fenway faithful. The crowd went nuts, dancing in the aisles and singing along with Mitch...er, Kevin, Millar.

Manager Terry Francona happened upon Millar and his buddy Manny Ramirez striding purposefully through the underground passageways of Minnesota's Metrodome the morning of a game against the Twins. Francona asked where the dynamic duo were going. "We're going to pray for hits," said Millar. "Whoa!" replied the manager. "Take along a lightning rod."

Kevin Millar, here during the 2004 ALCS, was the clubhouse prankster who also came up with numerous key hits and plays during the magical 2004 season.

Kevin Millar has many loyal buddies on the Red Sox, but during the 2004 ALCS and World Series, apparently no one was more reliable than Jack Daniels. In case you don't know, Jack, or Old No. 7 as he is sometimes known, is a mellow chap with lots of spirit. He hails from Lynchburg, Tennessee.

After the Red Sox had won the 2004 World Series, team members appeared on many TV shows. On Fox Sports Net's *Best Damn Sports Show Period,* Millar stated, "Before starting Game 6 [of the ALCS against the Yankees], it was about 35 degrees out there at Yankee Stadium. I went around and got a thing of Jack Daniels and we all did shots of Jack Daniels about 10 minutes before the game. And we won Game 6. So Game 7, of course, we had to do shots of Jack Daniels. And we won Game 7, so guess what? I'm glad we won in Game 4 [of the World Series sweep] because these Crown Royal shots and Jack Daniels shots started to kill me. And that's how the Sox did it." He went on to say, "Can you imagine [Red Sox manager] Terry Francona taking a shot of Crown Royal before Game 4 of the World Series? It's all out there now, baby. We were drunk."

Asked if any players had shown signs of impairment, he said, "Trot Nixon was. He swung 3–0 and had a take sign with bases loaded and hit the ball off the wall. He was supposed to take that pitch."

Millar later revised his comments in a conversation with ESPN's Hall of Fame reporter Peter Gammons. "I wish I'd never opened my mouth," he said, presumably referring to the comments rather than the consumption of the whiskey. "It was one of those group team things, like shaving our heads last year. What we had was one small Gatorade cup, with a little Jack Daniels in it. We passed it around and everyone symbolically drank out of the same cup because we are a team. It wasn't as if guys were drunk."

After the unbridled joy of 2004, several of the Red Sox heroes went into slumps in 2005. Millar was one of those players. In 2003 Millar had hit 25 homers for the Red Sox, and in 2004 he contributed 18. However, going into an August 24 contest with the Royals in Kansas City, he had gone 182 at-bats without hitting a home run and had only four on the season. So when he finally broke out of his dry spell with a second-inning homer off D. J. Carrasco on a 1–0 pitch, it should have been cause for celebration. But this is the Boston Red Sox and they do things just a little bit differently.

As Millar was making his home run trot around the bases, his "friend" David Ortiz conspired with the rest of the Red Sox players to completely ignore Millar when he returned to the dugout. Usually this rite of initiation is reserved for rookies who have just hit their first major league homer. Ortiz, Schilling, and company did not even acknowledge his existence as he came down the steps. Finally, the conspiracy fell apart as Jason Varitek and others could restrain themselves no longer and pummeled their popular teammate. Soon, everyone was clapping him on the back and banging him on his batting helmet. As for Millar, the biggest jokester and instigator of the group, he was philosophical. "I deserved it," he said. "I didn't expect any applause after not hitting a homer for so long."

Throughout the long slump, Millar tried to maintain his sense of humor. When the Red Sox played the Rangers, outfielder Lew Ford, who hails from Millar's hometown of Beaumont, Texas, robbed him of a home run with a great catch. When Ford singled in the next inning, the two home boys had the following exchange at first base:

Ford: "You're my favorite player."

Millar: "Thanks a lot...what are you doing to me!?"

In an effort to explain his home run drought, Millar compared his situation to that of another Boston athlete who wins despite less than outstanding stats. "It's just like Tom Brady," he said, referring to the three-time Super Bowl quarterback of the New England Patriots. "If you had a fantasy football draft, he'd be your eighth, ninth, tenth quarterback picked. You'd want to take Daunte Culpepper, and you'll finish in third place. You want to take [Michael] Vick and Peyton Manning and all these guys. I may not hit a home run the rest of the year and we might win the World Series. And I'm part of this team. Somehow, somewhere, I bring something."

A few weeks later, a Tom Brady jersey mysteriously appeared in Millar's locker, onto which was taped a newspaper account of his statement. Millar donned the jersey and wore it to the field for fielding practice. A football was offered him and he spent several minutes demonstrating his quarterbacking skills. Lest you think such stunts might land him in hot water with Red Sox management, it was none other than general manager Theo Epstein and manager Terry Francona who had set him up. Just to let everyone know, Millar also sported a headband clearly labeled THEO.

Millar continued his resurgence and broke out of his home run slump in style on August 31 in a game against the Tampa Bay Devil Rays, hitting two home runs to lead the Red Sox to a come-from-behind 7–6 win over the D-Rays. The second homer came off Jesus Colome's 96-mile-per-hour fastball and struck three-quarters up the Coke bottle beyond the Green Monster. Millar's biggest booster has always been his mother, a blonde bombshell of enthusiasm who is proud of her son. After the Tampa Bay game, Millar confessed that his mom has been less vocal during the slump. "She's been incognito," he claimed. "I haven't been her son."

The Reebok shoe company sent T-shirts to Manny Ramirez with block lettering that said: "Manny Being Manny." Millar, who claims to have coined the phrase was seen wearing the shirt in the Red Sox clubhouse and complaining of the unfairness of life. "I say this [stuff] and he's getting the profits," he moaned. "I'm getting snubbed. 'Cowboy Up.' Then 'Manny Being Manny.' Reebok will make $1.5 million and I'll be back in Beaumont going paycheck to paycheck."

Doug Mirabelli: Butterfly Catcher

Baseball has become a highly specialized sport. Nowhere is that more evident than in the case of Doug Mirabelli, personal catcher for Tim Wakefield. Whenever the knuckleballer is scheduled to pitch, Mirabelli dons his tools of ignorance and spends his time trying to net the baseball butterflies that Wakefield releases into the wild.

But Mirabelli is more than just Wakefield's caddy. The talented backup to Jason Varitek may just be the best second banana backstop in the game today. In fact he could be a starting catcher for many major league teams. The muscular 6'1", 205-pound product of Kingman, Arizona, catches and calls a good game, possesses a strong and accurate arm to second, and has some pop in his bat. On a game against the Tampa Bay Devil Rays on August 31, 2005, he showed another side of his game. With two out in the bottom of the seventh inning, Mirabelli, who had homered earlier in the game, reached base with a walk. Mirabelli then did the unthinkable, something so unusual and shocking that it was akin to Johnny Damon getting a buzz cut or Trot Nixon sporting a brand new fedora in right field. The plodding, foot-stuck-in-molasses, elephant-trotting catcher took off for second. D-Rays' pitcher Jesus Colome, totally concentrating on the batter and giving Mirabelli about as much attention as the guy in row 36 of the right-field bleachers, didn't see the move until "Motorin' Mirabelli" was scant feet from second. He finally turned and threw, but Doug the Slug slid in just ahead of the throw. "I don't know how they didn't see him," said manager Terry Francona after the game, "because I *felt* him." It was Mirabelli's second swipe of the season, a career high (he has three career steals to date) that must have left Rickey Henderson quaking in his boots. After the game, the catcher explained his strategy. "I don't do the team a lot of good on first base," he said. "I can't score from second on a double. It's got to be in the triangle, even at second."

Bill Mueller: Player's Player

Bill Mueller is your friendly neighborhood third baseman. Like Spider-Man, he is an unassuming gentleman by day, but when he slips into his uniform each evening, he spreads his defensive web around third base and defies hitters to get the ball past him. At the plate he is consistent and sometimes brilliant, as evidenced by his American League batting title in 2003 (.326 average).

On July 29, 2003, Bill Mueller made baseball history. He became the only player to hit grand slams from both sides of the plate in the same game. He had warmed up to the task by hitting a solo homer left-handed in the third inning of the 14–7 drubbing of the Texas Rangers off R. A. Dickey. In the seventh he moved to the other side of the plate and hit his first bases-loaded drive off reliever Aaron Fultz. The very next inning he came to bat again with the bases jammed. This time, batting from the left side, he homered again off Jay Powell. The nine RBIs were his career high. Despite the enormity of his feat, Mueller was his usual modest self after the game. "You never come to the ballpark thinking you're going to do anything like this," he said. "It didn't turn out like an ordinary night. I'm very humbled by this."

Trot Nixon: Blue-Collar Hero

At the end of a baseball season, Trot Nixon's baseball cap resembles a dishrag left overnight in a bowl of bleach. Or perhaps it looks more like the target of some wayward seagulls from Boston Harbor—or, more likely, New York Harbor. Or, more appropriately, like it was stone-washed in the "muddy waters of the River Charles." No longer is it a crisp shade of dark blue set off by a crimson "B." It is a shapeless, sweat-stained, off-whitish, shapeless piece of cloth that no self-respecting haberdasher would offer to the public. But Boston has always loved blue-collar players, and Trot is one of the original "Dirt Dogs." It is the color of the hat, not the collar, that proves it. He is all business, all the time.

It was Nixon's hard hat—i.e., batting helmet—that finally got him in hot water in October of 2004 when officials from Major League Baseball threatened to fine him for hiding the Red Sox logo under a sticky coating of pine tar and resin.

"It's an absolute joke," a defiant Nixon told the *Boston Globe*'s Gordon Edes. "I don't care what they say, I'm not paying any fine." He went on to explain the reason for the resin. "If you put resin on your bat, say it's 32 ounces, and you're using the same bat for, say three weeks, it will keep getting heavier. And all of a sudden you'll say to yourself, 'What in the world is going on with this bat? Why is it so heavy? I got [the idea of tapping his hands on the top of his resin-coated helmet] from Manny [Ramirez]. He told me to do it...I was like, 'Hey, he's got a point.'"

In April 2000 Trot Nixon's wife Kathryn ran the Boston Marathon. While the famous race was going on, the Red Sox were losing 1–0 to the Oakland A's at Fenway. After the game, Trot hurried to the finish line to congratulate his wife on completing the arduous race. Kathryn finished in just under four hours, a very respectable showing. As Nixon sought her out in the milling crowd to congratulate her, Red Sox fans among the runners recognized him and stopped to ask how the Red Sox had done that day. "We lost," he replied. "Now shouldn't you cross the finish line?"

On July 15, 2005, the Boston Red Sox demolished the New York Yankees 17–1 at Fenway Park. It was one of those nights when everything went right for Boston and everything went wrong for the Yanks. For example, Trot Nixon, not exactly the most likely candidate to hit an inside-the-park home run, did just that. Nixon hit the ball towards Melky Cabrera in center field and as the usually sure-handed fielder charged the ball, it bounced and, according to Nixon, "took a hard right." The ball rolled all the way to the wall, allowing Nixon to score standing up. Manny Ramirez and David Ortiz scored ahead of him. It was Nixon's first inside-the-parker in 20 years, one of 15 hits pounded out by the Bosox. The last one came when he was 11 years old and earned him a pair of Air Jordans from his mother, Sandy. "She told me she'd buy me some new Air Jordans if I hit an inside-the-park home run," Nixon recalled after the game. "And she did. I won't be getting any Air Jordans tonight. I'll just get an oxygen mask."

Hideo Nomo: Nomo Throws a No-No

As the first Japanese star to make it big as a pitcher in the major leagues, Hideo Nomo was already a pioneer. Little did he know that in April 2001, his first game in a Boston Red Sox uniform, he would join the elite of the Major League Baseball fraternity. Nomo was just hoping that his debut in Boston would be successful after several disappointing seasons in which he jumped from team to team. He began his career in 1995 as a member of the Los Angeles Dodgers and responded by being named National League Rookie of the Year. On September 17 of the following year, he pitched a no-hitter against the Colorado Rockies. On April 4, 2001, Nomo, now a member of the Red Sox, threw another no-no, this time against the Baltimore Orioles. He became only the fourth pitcher to turn the trick in both the National and American Leagues. Cy Young, Jim Bunning, and Nolan Ryan were the others.

John Olerud: Professional Hit Man

Well before joining the Boston Red Sox, John Olerud had built a reputation as a man who lets his actions speak louder than the precious few words he utters. In his 16 major league seasons, the 6'5", 225-pound first baseman accumulated a record that any major leaguer would be proud of.

Originally selected by the Toronto Blue Jays in the third round of the 1989 amateur draft, the left-handed hitter played eight seasons in Toronto. He then moved to the New York Mets (1997–1999), the Seattle Mariners (2000–2004), and the New York Yankees (2004) before being signed to a minor league contract by the Red Sox in May 2005. He was recovering from career-threatening surgery to repair torn ligaments in his left foot. Up to that point, Olerud had been one of those rare players—the others are Bob Horner and Dave Winfield—who never played a game in the minor leagues, at least not until he was sent to Pawtucket at the ripe old age of 37. He was hardly in awe of Triple A pitchers. His first hit was a home run and he batted .300 in 10 at-bats. Johnny O, who is keeping his Pawtucket jersey as a souvenir, saw the experience as just another part of his résumé, albeit a bit out of sync. "Guys used to say I didn't have any minor league stories to tell," he said. "They can't say that anymore."

Olerud's smooth, effortless swing is a thing of beauty and could be used as a template for all major league hitters. He owned a .295 batting mark, with 248 homers going into the 2005 season. His most outstanding season came in 1993 when he made a run for .400, finishing with a lofty .363 average, a .473 on-base percentage, and a league-best 54 doubles. The quest for a .400 average sparked comparisons with Ted Williams, although Williams was quick to point out that their swings were actually quite different. However, Olerud did resemble Ted in his patience at the plate and his desire to "get a good ball to hit," Ted's mantra. He certainly instilled Ted-like respect in the minds of rival pitchers, tying Ted's American League record (set in 1957) for intentional walks with 33. He also hit 24 homers, garnered 200 hits, and drove in 107 runs, all career highs, as he led the Blue Jays to a World Series Championship. It was the second of two back-to-back world championship teams that he played for north of the border.

Olerud wears a batting helmet at the plate and on the field, a result of a brain aneurysm he suffered at Washington State University, where he was a pitcher. He still possesses a strong and accurate throwing arm. The two-time All-Star is also a great defensive player and has captured three Gold Glove awards.

If Olerud is ever thrown out at home plate on a close play after being waved in by third base coach Dale Sveum, don't expect dissension in the Red Sox ranks. Sveum and Olerud are cousins.

David Ortiz: Papi Knows Best

The signing of David Ortiz from the Minnesota Twins for $1.25 million may go down in history as a stroke of genius. Certainly his home run swing is a stroke of hitting genius, an educated, practiced, grooved swing that sends baseballs huge distances. In his first full year in Boston, one of the few players who were not surprised by Ortiz' offensive output was Pedro Martinez. "I've know David for a long time," said Pedro. "I always knew he could hit." Now the rest of the American League pitchers know what Pedro knew.

If 6'4", 230-pound left-handed hitting Ortiz reminds you of former 6'1", 230-pound left-handed hitting Red Sox slugger Mo Vaughn, you're

David Ortiz, here knocking in the winning run in the fourteenth inning in Game 5 of the championship series, keyed the Red Sox's comeback against the Yankees in the 2004 ALCS. He was also instrumental in helping the Red Sox get to the postseason three years in a row by clouting 119 home runs.

not alone. Many fans have commented on the similarities. As it turns out, the connection between the two goes beyond physicality. "I used to watch Big Mo hit here [at Fenway]," Ortiz told *Boston Baseball* writer John Tomase in the July 2003 issue. "We always talked and he tried to teach me. He said everything he tried to do was hit the Green Monster. When you hit that way, you have to stay closed. And when the pitchers see you trying to do it and they come inside, you've got different choices." Thank you, Mo!

Writer Ray Duckler of the *Concord Monitor* had an apt description of Ortiz' hitting prowess to all fields. "He's Rod Carew with power," said Duckler.

In his or her heart, every Red Sox fan has known for some time that David Ortiz is Mr. Clutch. And now, it's official. Ortiz won yet another ballgame with a walkoff homer on September 6, 2005, against the California Angels. The home run came in the midst of the Red Sox drive for the American League East title, with the Yankees only three games back in the standings. The Red Sox principal owner John W. Henry presented Ortiz with a plaque, designed by team vice chairman Phil Morse, that contained the inscription: "David Ortiz, #34, The Greatest Clutch Hitter in the History of the Boston Red Sox."

Until the latest homer, the Red Sox had intended to make the presentation in private, a kind of personal recognition of a public fact. But Henry was so impressed with Ortiz that he decided to go public. "I said 'Let's do it.' I couldn't wait any longer. David is the best hitter I've ever seen when the game is on the line. He's also probably one of the nicest guys that has ever been in the clubhouse." The owner went on to say, "I'm very happy to declare publicly what almost all of us in New England already know: David Ortiz is the greatest clutch hitter to ever wear the uniform of the Boston Red Sox. I say 'almost' because beginning [today] the debate will begin."

The walk-off homer that prompted the presentation was a jack worthy of a plaque. The fact that it was the winner of a key game during a stretch drive would have made it huge even if it had barely cleared the right-field fences, but this blast was huge in every way. It landed in the alley that separates the bleachers and grandstand in right field. Angels

TOP TEN

Significant Homers by David Ortiz

1. October 17, 2004—Twelfth inning, off Paul Quantrill in 6–4 win over Yankees*
2. October 8, 2004—Tenth inning, off Jarrod Washburn in 8–6 win over Angels**
3. September 23, 2003—Tenth inning, off Kurt Ainsworth in a 6–5 win over Orioles
4. September 14, 2005—Eighth inning, off Josh Towers in a 5–3 win over the Blue Jays that kept the Red Sox 2½ games ahead of the Yankees
5. September 12, 2005—Eleventh inning, off Pete Walker in 6–5 win over Blue Jays; it was Ortiz' second homer of the night and the 40th of the season (gave Red Sox 3½-game lead over the Yankees)
6. September 6, 2005—Ninth inning, off Scot Shields in 3–2 win over Angels
7. June 2, 2005—Ninth inning, off B. J. Ryan in 6–4 win over Orioles
8. April 11, 2004—Twelfth inning, off Aquilino Lopez in 6–4 win over Jays
9. September 20, 2005—Ortiz homers twice to spark Red Sox to a 15–2 rout of Tampa Bay
10. Yet to come—The "walk-off on water" homer

*in ALCS
**in ALDS

right fielder Vladimir Guerrero, a friend of Ortiz, did not move a muscle, only his eyes following the ball as it left the park in a split second. "He's coming home with me tonight," said Ortiz. "I'll ask him how far it went."

The next day, a fan named Greg Rybarczyk, the developer of a home run measuring device called Hit Tracker, announced that the ball traveled an estimated 457 feet, the longest drive of the 2005 season at Fenway. He also reported that the ball left the bat at a speed of 122.5 mph and that it attained a maximum height of 120 feet in the air. Ortiz was characteristically modest about the feat. "It's a good feeling, especially when you have a guy like Wakefield out there performing the way he did tonight. You want to do something for the guy. I felt terrible the one inning that I struck out with men on second and third. When the game is on the line, you get another chance, you have to bring everything you have."

As to the distance the ball traveled, Wakefield was the winner but lost out as a prognosticator. "I told Manny [Ramirez], 'You're going to win this thing.' And he said, 'No, David said he was going to win it for us.'"

When Ortiz crossed home plate he was enveloped in a swarm of jubilant teammates. "Yeah, dude," said Ortiz. "You have to [take off the helmet], otherwise they beat me up. Trot Nixon and [Kevin] Millar and [Doug] Mirabelli, they smack you. They hit like Tyson out there."

On September 20, 2005, Ortiz hit two home runs to lead the Red Sox to a much needed 15–2 laugher over the Devil Rays in Tampa Bay. One of the homers, his 46th of the season, landed in a children's playground area 451-feet from home plate. Teammate John Olerud offered the following advice: "Maybe they ought to put out a public address announcement to tell those children out there to be careful."

At 6'4", 230-pounds, Ortiz isn't exactly built for speed, so when he caught the California Angels flat-footed by bunting in the eighth inning of a 5–1 Red Sox victory on August 21, 2005, it got everyone's attention. No one was more amused than Ortiz himself. "I was kind of nervous when I thought about it," he said later. Although he will never be mistaken for Rickey Henderson, the slugger was coy when asked if he might bunt again. "You never know, you never know," he said. "We've got a new lead-off man," chimed in teammate Edgar Renteria. Manager Terry Francona was less enthusiastic about Ortiz' role as a table-setter. "We don't want him to bunt 30 times a season," he said with a smile.

On August 12, 2005, David Ortiz hit two home runs to carry the Red Sox to a 9–8 win over the Chicago White Sox, who at that point had the best record in baseball. Well, he had to, didn't he? That morning a little boy had his picture taken with his hero and said, "You're going to hit two home runs tonight." Even for Ortiz, this seemed like a tall order, as he related to *Globe* writer Gordon Edes. "I said, 'Whoo—I don't know about that,'" said the popular Dominican. After he had hit one over the Green Monster and drove another over the center-field barrier, Ortiz was giving the kid's powers of prophecy more respect. "I'm going to have to look for that guy tomorrow and see what he's got for me," he said with a broad grin. Ortiz had been the victim of some bad luck before the two-homer outburst, hitting balls right at fielders or being robbed of hits by great fielding plays. "The way he swung the bat tonight, you don't rob those," said manager Terry Francona after the game, "unless an usher wanted to go and get it."

Commenting on Ortiz' penchant for game-winning heroics, no less an authority than the *New York Times* gushed (yes, the staid *New York Times* actually gushed like a down market tabloid), "[Ortiz is] maybe more terrifying than any hitter on the planet." This elevation of Papi to a kind of secular "Papicy" knows no end. You can almost envision him arriving for his at-bats in a Papi-mobile à la Pope John Paul II. Canonized? That's the way pitchers feel after Papi hits one.

Of course, Papi already has an airplane named after him. Delta Air Lines Inc.'s Song affiliate has rechristened a Boeing 757 "Big Papi" in his honor.

It seems that Ortiz has almost as many nicknames as clutch hits. Born David Americo Ortiz Arias on November 18, 1975, it is little wonder that teammates and fans prefer to call him something shorter. Perhaps the most prevalent of his monikers are "Papi," "Señor Papi," or "Big Papi," a tribute to both his imposing physical presence and his gentle demeanor. He is sometimes called "Cookie Monster" for similar reasons. Since the number-three hitting Ortiz and clean-up hitter Manny Ramirez are often referred to as "thunder and lighting," "Thunder" would be another de facto nickname. But perhaps the most bizarre appellation of all is "Flo." It seems that some of his more imaginative teammates spotted a facial resemblance to actress Esther Rolle, who played a character called Florida Evans on the TV sitcom *Good Times*. Whatever you call him, you can always call him "clutch."

The only miraculous finish left is for Papi to walk-off on water!

MVP Debate

A fierce debate raged during the 2005 American League pennant races over whether a designated hitter such as David Ortiz deserved the same kind of consideration for MVP honors as a position player such as Alex Rodriguez of the Yankees or Vladimir Guerrero of the Los Angeles Angels of Anaheim. There were arguments on both sides of the issue. Here are pro and con opinions on the issue.

PRO: Hal Bodley on USAToday.com: "If the Red Sox, atop the AL East virtually the entire season, didn't have Ortiz, they would not be holding that lofty perch. He's hands down the team leader, in the clubhouse and on the field....Ortiz gets my vote."

PRO: Don Baylor (former MVP and often DH for the '79 Angels): "I've always viewed it like this," he told Hal Bodley. "If you take a player away from a team, where does it finish? Ortiz has meant so much to the Red Sox. When the game's on the line, I know who they'd like to have up there to win it. A-Rod is surrounded by a lot of stars and can be pitched around from time to time. With Ortiz, he's a force."

CON: Tom Verducci on SI.com: "Ortiz doesn't play defense. There is no way to understate this. The guy is half a player. He is a specialist. He can devote his entire energies to his at-bats. There is a good reason why no position player ever has won the MVP with fewer than 97 games in the field (Don Baylor, 1979). A DH would have to be miles better than the next player who actually contributes to his team in both halves of the game."

CON: Blue Jays pitcher Josh Towers, after losing a game on a Ortiz homer: "I could never vote for a guy who doesn't play defense. They don't go through the grind other guys go through defensively, diving after balls, chasing balls. If you make an error, it might affect you, but if you're a DH, you don't go through any of that. You just hit."

Ortiz: "As soon as they bring my name up [for MVP consideration], they say, 'Oh, he's a DH. I don't think he deserves it because he's a DH.' That's fine with me. I never saw anybody win the MVP because he won the Gold Glove and hit .230. You win the MVP because you help your ball-club, you win games whenever your team needs it, and because you put up some numbers."

And the winner is...

Alex Rodriguez

Manny Ramirez: Manny Being Manny

We've heard of "going over the Wall," and with his awesome power to left, he has done it many times at Fenway, but Manny Ramirez has recently made a habit of going AWOL *through* the Wall, disappearing behind the green door of the scoreboard in Fenway's famous left-field barrier during home games. He emerges about three minutes later to cheers from the fans down the left-field line. What does he do back there? Your guess is as good as ours, but there isn't much in the way of creature comforts in the cramped quarters, just a sweaty scoreboard man and stacks of numbers waiting to announce scoring changes.

During a game on July 18, 2005, against Tampa Bay, Ramirez made his usual exit between pitches by Red Sox starter Wade Miller. He barely made it back to the field, and was still moving toward his position, when Miller delivered his next pitch. Thankfully for Manny, the batter, Joey Gathright, took the pitch, but he singled to left on the very next offering, causing much conjecture amongst the Fenway Faithful about whether Gathright could have managed an inside-the-park homer on the little bloop hit. Miller was later asked if he had considered checking to see if his left fielder was present on the field, something like asking if he checked to see if the Citgo sign was still standing. "Why would I check?" he reasonably responded. Should he have to ask for a show of hands of all those present and accounted for between each pitch? The missing Manny gave a whole new meaning to the term "eight men out," since he arbitrarily altered Abner Doubleday's (or was it Alexander Cartwright's) concept of the game.

Just two days previous, Manny had also disappeared into the mouth of the Green Monster during a pitching change against the Yankees. That was less stressful for all concerned, but he returned in plenty of time and with a wave to his left-field admirers. Of course, his actions beg the question: What does he do back there? The answer, according to Manny, is "I [peed] in a cup." How can you do that when 35,000 people are watching and waiting? Manager Terry Francona was philosophical about his AWOL fielder. "I'm just glad he came back," he said. Apparently manager, starting pitcher, and Manny were all—in their own way—relieved.

While Manny was on the bench as trade rumors swirled around Fenway days prior to the trade deadline at the end of July 2005, Kevin Millar took over his place in left. In a strange tribute to his teammate and friend, Millar made a move to disappear through the Green Monster door. He then mimicked Ramirez' famous two-arm disco pointing motion. Fans along the left-field line joined in the Red Sox Nation imitation urination celebration.

Red Sox longtime announcer Jerry Remy refers to Manny's sometimes inexplicable on-field exploits as JMBM, or Just Manny Being Manny.

One of the best hitters, maybe of all time, outfielder Manny Ramirez, here celebrating the Red Sox World Series victory, joined the Red Sox in 2001 and has been an All-Star every year, including 2002 when he led the league in hitting at .349.

Say it ain't so, Manny! In the year 2000, Pacific Trading Cards released a set of cards that included thin slices of game-used bats of major league stars. Two hobby retailers claimed that they discovered cork on the pieces of bat once used by Manny Ramirez. Pacific's PR man confirmed that cork was indeed found in Manny's bat when it was being cut. Evan Kaplan of the Major League Baseball Players Association's trading cards and memorabilia division was quick to point out that there was "no evidence it came directly from Manny...[and]...no evidence that it was his bat."

Ramirez has been referred to as a hitting savant. He appears to have an ability to set the agenda with an opposing pitcher. Teammate Johnny Damon is convinced that he sometimes takes an awkward or off-balance swing in order to encourage the pitcher to throw the same pitch again, this time with him lying in wait for it like an alligator feigning injury. Former Sox reliever Alan Embree claims that he's seen Ramirez swing at ball three in order to set up the pitcher. On another occasion, he recalled, "Manny looked really bad on a curveball. He wasn't even close. So the guy throws him another one, even better, and Manny just crushes it into orbit. Manny suckered the guy. He just acted like the first one fooled him." Call it Manny being canny. Whatever you call it, these kinds of hitting smarts are usually associated with guys like Ted Williams, Ty Cobb, or Wade Boggs.

Ramirez once asked the clubhouse boy to wash his car and told him that he would find enough money in the glove compartment to cover the cost. The astonished youth found in excess of $10,000, enough for a nice wax job too. It took $160 million, spread over eight seasons, for the Red Sox to pry Manny from the Cleveland Indians. When Pedro Martinez was about to depart for New York, Manny offered to use some of this money to keep Pedro in Boston.

Manny Ramirez has been the centerpiece for many bizarre happenings at Fenway Park. Just before baseball's trading deadline at 4:00 PM on the last day of July 2005, it looked as if Manny might become a member of the New York Mets. So when he emerged from the dugout to pinch-hit in the eighth inning of a tie game against the Twins, the Boston crowd went wild with cheers. This was the same Fenway Park that had reverberated with a combination of cheers and boos for Manny just two days earlier when it looked like he would leave the Red Sox—for—wait for it—more "privacy" in New York. After changing his "I vant to be alone" attitude, Manny the pinch-hitter promptly singled up the middle to drive in what was to be the winning run in a 4–3 Red Sox victory. Earlier in the week, manager Terry Francona had pondered life with Manny in Red Sox Nation. "Is it always *Mr. Rogers' Neighborhood*?" he asked rhetorically "No. It's grownups playing, and once in a while you have to get a little agitated." But when Manny is happy, it really is a beautiful day in the neighborhood.

Before the Twins–Red Sox game of July 31, a game during which the non-waiver deadline would arrive, Sox court jester/UN diplomat Kevin Millar led Manny into Terry Francona's office and announced that Ramirez had something to say. Manny expressed his desire to stay in Boston. Meanwhile, Millar acted as his official translator, speaking gibberish in the background as Manny, in perfectly satisfactory English, made his conciliatory statement. "I want to be with this team and win another World Series," said Ramirez, ensuring that nothing was lost in translation.

Just when you thought things couldn't get any stranger, Manny was reportedly wearing Oakley sunglasses in left field. So what, you ask? Well, Oakley's have a built in MP3 player. No wonder he marches to a different tune.

During the red-hot American League East division race, it seemed that David Ortiz came through with clutch hits at least once a week to lift the Red Sox to victory. Not to be outdone, Manny Ramirez, who bats fourth behind Papi in the powerful Sox lineup, proceeded to win two games in a row against the Oakland A's with consecutive game-winning hits, one more painful than the other, but both equally effective.

The first came on September 16, with the Red Sox clinging to a narrow 1½-game lead over the Yankees. The score was 2–2 in the bottom of the tenth frame at Fenway. The Red Sox had loaded the bases with just one out. The Athletics flooded the infield with five defensive players, trying to choke off the winning run. They had prepared for every contingency save one, the seldom seen walk-off HBP. The 1–1 pitch from A's reliever Keiichi Yabu plunked Manny in the left elbow, driving in the winning run. Manny was quite willing to take one for the team, but in his mixture of joy and pain he almost forgot to touch first base to make things official. The Red Sox charged from the dugout to celebrate Manny's RBI, making for a strange dynamic. "Here I am running like a goofball, all happy, and Manny is wincing in pain," said Johnny Damon after the game, before adding, "It's awesome!"

The next night Manny won a game in the more conventional—and less painful manner—with a sixth-inning home run off Dan Haren that broke a 1–1 tie and provided the margin of victory as the Sox beat the A's 2–1.

TRIVIA

Which member of the 2005 Boston Red Sox penned a book titled *Idiots*?

Answers to the trivia questions are on pages 175–176.

Edgar Renteria

As a member of the St. Louis Cardinals, Edgar Renteria recorded the final out of the 2004 World Series against the Red Sox, little did he know that he would be playing for the reigning world champs the next spring. He also made the last out—this time as a fielder on the victorious teams—for the 1997 World Series champion Florida Marlins. Such is the nature of baseball.

The usually sure-handed fielder was a disappointment for the Red Sox in 2005. He committed a career-high 30 errors and had many Red Sox fans wondering why management had ever gotten rid of Orlando Cabrera, who had only 7 miscues for the L.A. Angels of Anaheim.

Dave Roberts

Red Sox fans have memories like elephants. Unfortunately the memories are sometimes too selective, as is the case with Buckner's blunder, Grady's mental error, and Stanley's sinker. These personalities did much more than these single actions, and yet those things are what they will forever be associated with. And then there's Dave Roberts. He spent only one-half of a season as a member of the Boston Red Sox, but he will

TRIVIA

Which member of the 2005 Boston Red Sox penned a book titled *Perfect I'm Not: Boomer on Beer, Brawls, Backaches, and Baseball?*

Answers to the trivia questions are on pages 175–176.

forever be a Red Sox hero. "It has truly impacted my life," he told writer Bob Ryan in the *Boston Globe*. "People are often remembered for one thing in their career, whether it's good or bad. Fortunately for me, that stolen base is embedded in people's minds."

The stolen base. There is only one of note in Red Sox history, despite the many pilfered by guys like Tommy Harper. It happened in Game 4 of the 2004 American League Championship Series, or what is known locally as The Greatest Comeback in Baseball History. It was the ninth inning, and the Red Sox were trailing the series three games to none. Kevin Millar drew a walk and was lifted for the much speedier Roberts. Mariano Rivera was suddenly distracted; in fact, he seemed obsessed by Roberts' presence at first. He threw to first once, twice, three times. The second try was close, but by now Roberts had the information he needed. On the first pitch to Bill Mueller, Roberts exploded toward second and slid in head-first just ahead of the tag. Mueller then singled over second base to knot the score, and David Ortiz, the heavy artillery, shelled the Yankees with a game-winning homer in the twelfth.

They say that circumstances produce heroes, and Roberts had just become the Winston Churchill of the Red Sox. If he had been asked to describe what he had accomplished in Churchillian terms, he might have said: "We shall go on to the end, we shall fight in New York, we shall fight in Boston, we shall fight with growing confidence and growing strength everywhere, we shall defend our pride, whatever the cost may be, we shall fight on the base paths, we shall fight at home plate, we shall fight in the field and in the streets, we shall fight from the mounds; we shall *never* surrender." He did not make such a speech of course, none was necessary because he inspired the Red Sox with his actions. He showed that it would take blood, toil, tears, and sweat to overcome the ordeal ahead of them. As Winston put it, "You ask, what is our aim? I can answer in one word. It is victory."

Certainly the steal was Roberts' "finest hour."

Roberts had been obtained by the Red Sox a scant 10 minutes before the July 31 trading deadline. The importance of the trade was lost on all but the most keen of Red Sox observers because that was the same day that the beloved Nomar left town. The truth was the Red Sox had attained a secret weapon that could alter the course of Red Sox history. There was no need for secret code or elaborate signaling. Roberts knew what was expected of him. "Terry just looked down the dugout at me and winked and said, 'You know what to do,'" says Roberts. And he did know what to do. He had been studying the enemy's maneuvers. He had engaged in espionage of the most sophisticated kind. During a game on September 17, he had experimented against Rivera—in retrospect they were like basic training or war games, readying him for live ammo combat. He probed the reliever's defenses and spotted his weaknesses. In fact he—like Moe Berg before him—had even used videotape to study the enemy's moves. He now knew Mariano Rivera liked to hold the ball to freeze the runner.

Game 5 was Roberts' last as a member of the Boston Red Sox. He did not play in Games 6 or 7 and he was not used in the World Series. His contribution had already been made and it was huge. His World Series ring is well deserved. He is now and forever part of Red Sox history and lore.

Curt Schilling: Mound Warrior

Curt Schilling is a geek and he doesn't care who knows it. By now, every Red Sox fan should be aware of Curt Schilling's love affair with computers. He is a regular and passionate member of certain Red Sox websites and chat rooms, and his contributions are always thoughtful. But the nerddom doesn't end there. On the mound, Schilling is used to battling villains and evil empires. Usually they have names such as Posada, Jeter, A-Rod, Giambi, and Sheffield. But it turns out Schilling continues to

By the NUMBERS

3—Number of stitches put in Curt Schilling's foot before Game 6 of the 2004 ALCS against the Yankees (the doctor had practiced the procedure on a cadaver first).

1—Number of stitches that ripped away during the game, causing dramatic bloody sock.

Providing the Red Sox with probably the game's best one-two punch in 2004 (along with Pedro Martinez), Curt Shilling went 21–6 and posted the second-best ERA in the league. He also won three games in the 2004 postseason.

battle evil even when he leaves the mound. The names are different but the evil is just as intense.

The Red Sox ace is addicted to an online game called EverQuest (a kind of online incarnation of Dungeons and Dragons, for all you old-timers out there). "My first foray into Lower Guk was a lot of fun....One night I log in and there's a 55 level monk there. Great guy. He's been there for, like, 12 hours. No Raster—pop, despawn, pop, despawn—still no Raster." And you probably thought Manny was hard to understand!

Schilling's infatuation with EverQuest goes back to his days as a Philadelphia Phillie, when he and teammate Doug Glanville were team-mates. When Schilling was dealt to the Arizona Diamondbacks, Glanville hit two homers off him in a game. Glanville explained that the dingers were just revenge for Schilling's having helped to kill Bingbong, Glanville's beloved, dwarven paladin.

Some people hit homers for little kids in hospitals; some hit them to avenge Bingbong. Whatever works. "Not enough attention is paid to the off-the-field motivators that create nasty on-field grudges," Glanville told the ESPN's *Week in Review*. "I believe video atrocities top the list. Curt Schilling assassinated my lovable Dwarf Paladin in EverQuest, happily smiling as his character stood in the safety of the town guards. That can create serious internal friction. I believe that we need to analyze some of the video atrocities committed on PlayStation2, or Dreamcasts, or even Commodore 64, if we need to go back that far." And then, "Schill has to live with what he has done. He can tell whatever story he wants, but the facts are the facts. Bingbong was set up, led to an untimely death in the prime of his life for no other reason than pure malice. Things like that do not go unavenged. Sometimes it spills out into the field of play."

"C'mon dude," replied Schilling reasonably. "You ever hear of a cleric pulling in a group with a paladin? Anyone with a lick of sense in EQ could see right through [Glanville's] babbling and knows that he was the train conductor in that entire episode."

Yogi Berra was much easier to understand.

Schilling told Jeff Moyer in 2003 that he is "a warmonger at heart." He is a World War II buff, has a dog named Patton, and collects World War II memorabilia, including reportedly a German minesweeper.

Ironically, it was Curt Schilling who *stopped* the Red Sox's bleeding. The man whose bloody sock will forever symbolize the dramatic end of the Red Sox 86-year championship drought was the same man who staunched the open wound that had been festering in Boston for almost nine decades. The tourniquet that he applied came in the form of brave and brilliant pitching efforts in the 2004 ALCS and World Series.

Schilling came to Boston from Arizona with the confidence and purpose of a faith healer, minus the flashy suit and slicked back hair. He had absolute faith that the Red Sox could go all the way and he defied conventional medicine to make it happen. You could almost call the result miraculous.

Unlike Tom Lasorda who professed to bleed Dodger blue, Schilling does not claim to bleed Red Sox red, although the bloody sock that has become an icon of the 2004 season did not clash with the crimson logo emblazoned on his uniform. In fact, it was a perfect fashion statement for the man destined to start a winning trend in his adopted home.

Schilling is baseball's answer to General George S. Patton Jr. He is baseball's version of "Old Blood and Guts" himself. He has shed blood for the Red Sox's cause and he has shown a ton of intestinal fortitude in clutch situations. No retreat. No surrender. Full speed ahead. Damn the torpedoes.

Take no prisoners.

The very idea of comparisons with Patton are quickly brushed aside by Schilling, a military buff whose father is a veteran. The Red Sox ace has the national pastime in proper perspective. "That was war, this is just a game," he is quick to point out to reporters anxious to make the connection. But there is one area where Schilling and Patton could legitimately be linked. They are both master strategists. They both live by the credo: know your enemy. In Schilling's case, the enemy is any batter who steps in against him in a major league ballgame. The pitcher studies batters the way Patton studied troop movements. His maneuvers are designed to create confusion in the enemy ranks. His arsenal is impressive, but it is the execution that secures the win. When batters think he is going to charge through the front door with a fastball, he invariably comes in through the side with a curve, or lobs a grenade in the form of a splitter that explodes as it reaches the plate. When he is at his best, his accuracy rivals "smart" bombs. But it is the realm of psychological warfare that he excels. He is just smarter and better prepared than everybody else. Hitters go to the plate with negative thoughts; they don't know what to expect.

Adam Stern: Welcome to Fenway, eh?

On July at Fenway Park in the midst of a 17–1 thrashing of the hated New York Yankees, when there were a hundred things for Red Sox fans to cheer about, the Fenway faithful rose to acknowledge the first hit by a young Canadian kid named Adam Stern. What makes this so truly unique is the fact that no announcement was made to inform the fans of Stern's accomplishment, and no message had yet flashed on the scoreboard. The fans just knew. In what other ballpark in America could this have happened?

Jason Varitek: Leader

Varitek's arrival in Boston represents one of the best trades in Red Sox history. The catcher came to the Red Sox with pitcher Derek Lowe as

Jason Varitek, here during Game 5 of the 2004 ALCS, was a two-time All-Star at catcher for the Red Sox, where he's spent his entire career through 2005.

TOP TEN

Red Sox Prospects as Selected by
Baseball America on November 10, 2004

1. Hanley Ramirez, SS
2. Brandon Moss, OF
3. Jon Papelbon, RHP
4. Jon Lester, LHP
5. Anibal Sanchez, RHP
6. Dustin Pedrola, SS
7. Luis Soto, SS
8. Kelly Shoppach, C
9. Abe Alverez, LHP
10. Manny Delcarmen, RHP

part of a trade with Seattle that rivaled in one-sidedness the beads-and-trinkets deal supposedly used to acquire Manhattan. The trinket that the Red Sox sacrificed to get Varitek and Lowe was Heathcliff Slocumb. Meanwhile, Varitek is the cornerstone of the new Boston Red Sox, the one indispensable man in the lineup that took the Sox to World Series glory in 2004. The man they call "Tek" (there is no truth to the rumor that his alma mater, the Georgia Institute of Technology was changed to Georgia Tech in his honor), plays a position at which so-called intangibles become very tangible when the score is tallied. Jason's pitch calling and ability to work with a diverse group of Red Sox pitchers makes him invaluable. His hitting prowess—from both sides of the plate—makes him exceptional and places him in the forefront of the current crop of major league backstops. Varitek studies hitters and knows the strengths and weaknesses of his pitching staff.

It's widely believed that A's GM Billy Beane is a baseball genius and, thanks to the book *Moneyball*, he has become an icon of the new, young thinking in baseball. And yet, how do you explain this? Beane admits that if he had taken the position of GM with the Red Sox, he would have immediately traded Varitek and signed Mark Johnson, then a backup catcher with the Chicago White Sox.

Tim Wakefield

Step right up, ladies and gentlemen! Don't be shy. Step right up and see the amazing knuckleball? Is it a curve? No! Is it a fastball? No! Is it a slider, a screwball, or a sinker? No! This is baseball's freak pitch! So strange that it defies the imagination and challenges every known law of science. You'll shake your head in disbelief as you watch it dart and dodge and dip. You'll laugh out loud as hitter's try to make contact with it. You'll guffaw as the catcher tries to catch it.

Yes, it's the amazing knuckleball, baseball's best sideshow—and the leading purveyor of this pitch is with us today to astound and befuddle you with his incredible acts of prestidigitation. Watch him grip the ball like a raw egg, watch him push it slowly toward home plate as if he were playing toss with a four-year-old. Watch the ball proceed plate-ward with no rotation whatsoever! Watch as invisible air currents take it places that even its creator can't predict.

And, oh, ladies and gentlemen, keep your eyes glued to the batter! Watch as powerful sluggers are reduced to helpless buffoons. Watch as .350 hitters go 0-for-5 and swing at pitches two feet out of the strike zone. Yes, step right up, ladies and gentlemen, and see the amazing, astounding, astonishing knuckleballer in action.

If baseball were a carnival, the knuckleball would be the equivalent of the yak girl and Tim Wakefield would be the barker who entices the crowd to view his novelty. The knuckleball is as out of place as a shrunken head at the Academy Awards. Bringing in the knuckleballer in relief is like hiring the Keystone Cops to look after U.S. homeland security.

Even in an anachronistic game such as baseball, it stands out as an anachronism. It is the spitball without the spit, the eephus pitch without the fuss; it is the "funny one" that Uncle Joe always threw you on sunny summer afternoons, as in, "Watch out, Jimmy, here comes the funny one."

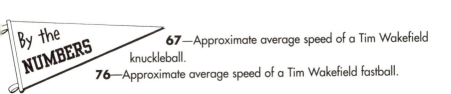

By the NUMBERS

67—Approximate average speed of a Tim Wakefield knuckleball.

76—Approximate average speed of a Tim Wakefield fastball.

Tim Wakefield is all but alone in his chosen profession, isolated—a veritable Wake island in a sea of conventional pitchers.

And yet Tim Wakefield is hardly a rebel. He is the ultimate team man, a player who gladly subordinates his own stats for the welfare of his teams. He is a conservative, family-oriented man whose idea of fun is to raise money for charity and occasionally jam with teammate Bronson Arroyo. In many ways, Tim Wakefield is the soul of the Boston Red Sox.

David Wells: Babe Ruth's Back

David Wells, the well-traveled member of the Red Sox pitching staff, is a huge (no joke intended) fan of Babe Ruth and used to wear Ruth's No. 3 on a T-shirt under his uniform. He was unable to wear Ruth's retired number but chose No. 33 as a tribute to his hero. When he came to the Red Sox he briefly wore No. 3, but eventually surrendered it to shortstop Edgar Renteria, who had worn it as a member of the St. Louis Cardinals.

Boomer, so named for his outsized physique (6'4", 225-pounds "officially"—nudge, nudge, wink, wink), outlandish behavior, and his outspoken ways, came to the Red Sox in a December 2004 deal after stops in various major league cities. He pitched a perfect game for the Yankees against Minnesota in 1998.

Kevin Youkilis: The Greek God of Walks

When Kevin Youkilis hit his first major league home run, the reception he got from teammates was underwhelming. "My first at-bat [that day], I just missed a pitch from hitting a home run," he told Ben Jacobs of *Hardball Times.* "I just got under a ball just enough, popped it up, just missed the pitch....Pedro [Martinez] watches the game pretty well. He saw that and he told me, 'When you hit a home run [at] your next at-bat, we're going to give you the silent treatment.' I was like, 'Yeah, right. I'm not going to hit a home run.' What do you know, I hit the ball and I knew it was gone right when I hit it. Spring around the bases and Crespo, the guy on deck, gave me a hug and I go back to the dugout and everybody was sitting in their seats, and I knew right then.

"It was funny, and everything was going so quick. Everything happens so quick when your adrenaline's up that high....I just went with it. That was kind of like my introduction to just being a part of the team."

The 50 Greatest Red Sox Players

Ranking is a mug's game. Anytime you try to rank anything, there are so many variables, mitigating circumstances, and subjective influences that the entire exercise becomes about as valid as my 12th-grade ID card. With that disclaimer in mind, it must also be said that ranking is a lot of fun, a great conversation starter, and for many—including myself—an obsession.*

The rankings below are mine. They are based on some solid statistical standards, some emotional influences, some mitigating factors, and some wild surmises. Players like Ruth, Foxx, and Eckersley, Hall of Famers all, may be ranked lower than you would like. All three also performed much of their careers for other ball clubs. Some, like Luis Tiant, may be ranked higher than mere statistics can justify. But if you ever saw Tiant pitch, and saw the impact he had on the team and on baseball, you would perhaps understand. Some players that, through no fault of their own, lost years to military service were also given special consideration for *what might have been.*

Knowing just how subjective these choices can be, I decided to ask good friend, fine writer, and fellow Red Sox fan John DeCoste to compile his own list, independent of mine, to serve as a kind of control group. We differed on the rankings—sometimes markedly—but basically agreed on the same top 50. That validated my choices, at least to me. John and I also agreed that everyone brings their own agenda to the task. Is longevity as worthy as a shorter but more spectacular career? Does a

*The author of this book once worked with Ted Williams on a book (*Ted Williams' Hit List*) that ranked the 20 greatest hitters of all time, so he is accustomed to being second-guessed, lectured, bullied, and admonished by the best of them. Take your best shot!

single season that helps the team end an 86-year championship drought catapult a player onto the list?

Here, for better or worse, are the 50 greatest Red Sox players of all time. I *dare* you to disagree. **

1. Ted Williams: The best hitter of all time. Period.
2. Carl Yastrzemski: A great all-around player, offensively and defensively.
3. Pedro Martinez: Smart, talented, passionate. The complete package. A power pitcher with finesse.
4. Roger Clemens: Power pitcher supreme. Statistically the best pitcher of his era, one of the best all-time.
5. Cy Young: 511 wins. The poster boy of pitching.
6. Tris Speaker: One of the all-time greats of baseball, offensively and defensively.
7. Harry Hooper: An unsung hero of major proportions.
8. Wade Boggs: Mr. Consistency. Just dial "B" for base hit.
9. Jim Rice: The most feared hitter in the AL during his prime years.
10. Luis Tiant: His starts were an event.
11. Jimmie Foxx: How can you deny such awesome power?
12. Fred Lynn: A natural hitter who could have been another Yaz.
13. Carlton Fisk: Produced the most-watched homer in baseball history.
14. Mel Parnell: The winningest left-hander in Red Sox history.
15. Jason Varitek: A leader on and off the field.
16. Babe Ruth: A great pitcher who could hit some, too.
17. Joe Cronin: Player, manager, and mentor.
18. Manny Ramirez: A hitting savant.
19. Lefty Grove: The passion to win.
20. Bobby Doerr: Nice guys can be winners.
21. Nomar Garciaparra: Brilliance denied.
22. David Ortiz: What a find! Before he finishes, he could be in the top 10.

** However, just in case you strongly disagree with one of the author's choices, and think that only an idiot would put him on the list, I deliberately threw a bogus selection into the mix. I'm sure I don't have to tell you who that is.

Nomar Garciaparra, here against Cleveland late in the 2003 season, was the heart and soul of the Red Sox for the seven and one-half seasons he played shortstop for them. A five-time All-Star, he was the league's Rookie of the Year in 1997 and led the American League in hitting in 1999 and 2000.

23. Dwight Evans: A great defensive right fielder.
24. Smoky Joe Wood: A fastball pitcher par excellence.
25. Frank Malzone: Our version of Brooks Robinson.
26. Dom DiMaggio: Belongs in the Hall of Fame.
27. George Scott: A slugger and prototype for Mo and Papi.
28. Dick Radatz: The first dominant.
29. Johnny Damon: Our salvation.
30. Johnny Pesky: Mr. Red Sox.
31. Mo Vaughn: Fearsome slugger.
32. Bill Lee: Colorful and competitive.
33. Rough Carrigan: One of the best Red Sox catchers.

34. Tim Wakefield: Predictably unpredictable.
35. Curt Schilling: For one year, but oh, what a year!
36. Duffy Lewis: One-third of baseball's great outfield.
37. Vern Stephens: Four-time All-Star while in Beantown.
38. Dutch Leonard: Underrated pitcher for championship teams.
39. Rico Petrocelli: Power-hitting infielder.
40. Jim Lonborg: Helped make Impossible Dream a reality.
41. Boo Ferriss: A brilliant star pitcher in a short career (65 wins–30 losses).
42. Pete Runnels: Two-time batting champ.
43. Billy Goodman: Batting champ.
44. Dennis Eckersley: Cocky but competent.
45. Tex Hughson: 96–54 record, three-time All-Star.
46. Jackie Jensen: Fragile superstar.
47. Wes Ferrell: As the old saying goes, "They elected the wrong Ferrell to the Hall of Fame." The pitcher even hit more homers than his catcher brother!
48. Mike Greenwell: A .303 career hitter with power.
49. Ellis Kinder: Ellis Kinder drunk was better than many pitchers sober.
50. Tony Conigliaro: As a symbol of what might have been.

Honorable mentions: Larry Gardner, Bob Stanley, Rick Ferrell, Bruce Hurst, Rick Burleson, Reggie Smith

Dom DiMaggio:
Hall of Famer-in-Waiting

One player who has not yet been enshrined in the National Baseball Hall of Fame in Cooperstown, but arguably should be, is Dom DiMaggio. In 1995 Ted Williams asked the author of this book to work with him to compose a letter endorsing and promoting Dom DiMaggio for the Hall of Fame. This is the letter that Ted sent to the veteran's committee. It shows the high esteem in which Ted held his former teammate. It also illustrates how truly difficult it is to make the Hall of Fame.

July 22, 1995
Dear Hall of Fame Veteran Committee member,

As a current member of the Hall of Fame and Veteran's Committee member, I am proud to put forth the name of my friend and teammate Dominick DiMaggio for Hall of Fame consideration. I feel privileged to nominate the "Little Professor" because if anyone deserves baseball's highest recognition, it is Dom. He is a man of great accomplishment and great character.

As a teammate of Dom's for eleven seasons with the Red Sox, I came to appreciate his contribution to baseball. He played the game with style and grace and always carried himself with quiet dignity on and off the field. In comparisons with his glamorous big brother, Joe, his achievements were often underrated or ignored, though his talent was recognized and applauded by everyone who knew the game. Dom could do it all: he ran the bases like a gazelle, he played a flawless center field, and he possessed a rifle arm (Enos Slaughter once confessed that he wouldn't have made his famous dash all the way home from first base in the '46 Series if Dom had been in center field). On top of all that, he was one of the best lead-off hitters in baseball. Most importantly, Dom was a great team player, always willing to sacrifice personal glory for the good of the team and, in fact, was the first Player's Representative for the Red Sox.

Dom was 5'9" and 168 lbs., about 90 percent of Joe's size and, as one writer pointed out, he was about 90 percent of the player Joe was. As Joe's biggest fan, I'd be the first to agree that Dom was no Joe DiMaggio, but that same writer (in John Thorn and Pete Palmer's Total Baseball) correctly suggests that "90 percent of Joe DiMaggio is better than 100 percent of most guys who've ever drawn major league salaries." Dom shouldn't be penalized for having a baseball icon in the family. His career must be considered on its own merit. Certainly Boston fans saw his value to the Red Sox when they sang, "He's better than his brother Joe, Dominick DiMaggio!"

I'm convinced that any fair and impartial assessment will place Dom in very select company indeed. Over eleven seasons Dom DiMaggio batted .298, with a slugging percentage of .419 and an on-base percentage of .383. He had 1,680 lifetime hits, 308 doubles, 57 triples, and 750 walks. Dom was a great lead-off man. He led the American League in runs scored twice—in 1950 with 131 and 1951 with 113. He also led the AL in triples in 1950 with 11, and that same year led the league in stolen bases with 15. He definitely had some pop in his bat, too. Hitting 87 homers and driving in 618 runs despite batting at or near the top of the batting order throughout his career. He holds the Red Sox record for the longest consecutive game-hitting streak with 34 in 1949—the ninth longest in AL history and in 1951 he hit safely in 27 consecutive games.

As a fellow hitter, I know how good Dom DiMaggio was at the plate. However, it's when you factor in his defensive and base-running skills that Dom becomes a superior candidate for Cooperstown. He stands fourth overall for center fielders in total chances-per-game, with a 2.99 average and chances-accepted-per-game, 2.92. He is also fourth in put outs per game with a 2.82 mark.

Dom excelled in all aspects of the game. He led the Red Sox in stolen bases five times—and he didn't do it for personal glory, he did it in key game situations, when we needed it most. I remember stepping into the batter's box and seeing him out there on second base. I remember him scoring ahead of me on countless occasions. I remember his grace and skill in the outfield. I still remember him throwing runners out with that gun of his. I remember all the so-called "little" things he did to win ballgames. Little wonder, he was chosen to the American League All-Star squad eight times, four times as a starter.

My induction into the Hall of Fame remains the proudest achievement of my baseball life. I was accorded that great honor because enough people decided in their minds and hearts that I deserved to be there. I am just as convinced in my own mind and in my own heart that Dom DiMaggio belongs in the Hall of Fame. Those who know me also know that Cooperstown represents a level of recognition that I would not bestow lightly. I am in Dom's corner all the way and I hope that, after careful consideration of his entire record, you will agree that his presence will only add to the prestige and the luster of this great American baseball shrine.

Yours sincerely,
Ted Williams
Hall of Fame Member, 1966

Red Sox Players in Baseball's Hall of Fame in Cooperstown

Wade Boggs—Inducted in 2005
Carlton Fisk—Inducted in 2000
Carl Yastrzemski—Inducted in 1989*
Bobby Doerr—Inducted in 1986*
Rick Ferrell—Inducted in 1984
Harry Hooper—Inducted in 1971
Red Ruffing—Inducted in 1967
Ted Williams—Inducted in 1966*
Joe Cronin—Inducted in 1956
Jimmie Foxx—Inducted in 1951
Herb Pennock—Inducted in 1948
Lefty Grove—Inducted in 1947
Jimmy Collins—Inducted in 1945
Cy Young—Inducted in 1937
Tris Speaker—Inducted in 1937
Babe Ruth—Inducted in 1936

*Played entire career as a member of the Red Sox

Joe Cronin was a player/manager for the Red Sox for more than a decade starting in 1935. With his bat, glove, and managerial acumen, he helped lead the Red Sox back to respectability.

The Red Sox Hall of Fame

In addition to the Hall of Fame in Cooperstown, the Boston Red Sox have their very own Red Sox Hall of Fame at Fenway Park to recognize those players and others who made the franchise one of the greatest in American sports history. It's well worth a visit.

The selection committee is made up of 15 executives and broadcasters, active and retired representatives of the media, and the Sports Museum of New England, as well as the Bosox Club. It hall opened its doors in1995.

Here are the players who are enshrined in the Boston Red Sox Hall of Fame (those players who are enshrined in Cooperstown are automatically included in the Red Sox Hall as well).

Wade Boggs, 3B (Red Sox 1982–1992)

Boggs was not yet enshrined in the Cooperstown club when he became a member of the Red Sox Hall of Fame in early 2004, but he is now. And how could he be denied? He was a veritable hitting machine during his time in Boston, as consistent as anyone who ever played the game. His career average as a member of the Red Sox was .338, bested only by Ted Williams, whose book, *The Science of Hitting*, became Boggs' batting bible. On four different occasions, Boggs batted over .360, winning five American League batting titles. He also collected 200 or more hits in seven consecutive seasons.

Inducted 2004

Rick Burleson, SS (Red Sox 1974–1980)

Rick Burleson was the prototypical hard-nosed shortstop. Known as the "Rooster" because of his cocky demeanor and aggressive attitude,

Burleson was the double-play king, executing more twin killings than any Red Sox shortstop before or since (and with players like Johnny Pesky and Nomar Garciaparra, there have been some great ones). He also maintains the major league single-season mark for most double plays turned by a shortstop (147 in 1980).

Inducted 2002

Tony Conigliaro, OF (Red Sox 1964–1967, 1969–1970, 1975)

When Tony C appeared on the major league scene with the Red Sox, he was the most exciting player to arrive in years. He hit a homer in his first Fenway at-bat and always seemed to come through in dramatic fashion. Conig was the youngest American Leaguer to hit 100 home runs. His career and his life almost came to a sudden end on August 18, 1967, when he was beaned by a fastball thrown by Jack Hamilton of the California Angels. Despite damage to his left eye, he made a courageous comeback, hitting 20 home runs and driving in 82 runs in 1969 as he was named Comeback Player of the Year. Conigliaro was the glamour boy of his day and had legions of fans, many of them female. Who's to say what he might have accomplished if he'd played out his career uninjured?

Inducted 1995

Dom DiMaggio, CF (Red Sox 1940–1942, 1946–1953)

A popular chant of the day said that he was better than his brother Joe, but even if he wasn't quite that good, Dom DiMaggio, the bespectacled man they called the "Little Professor" was a hell of a player. In center field his range and instincts rivaled his older brother, and Joe may hold the major league mark with a 56-game hit streak, but despite recent efforts by hitters such as Johnny Damon, Dom dominates the Red Sox list with his 34-game run. DiMaggio finished his career with a batting average just under .300 (.298), and no less an authority than teammate Ted Williams lobbied hard to have him inducted into the National Baseball Hall of Fame in Cooperstown. With Ted batting behind him, the perennial All-Star led the AL in runs scored in 1950 and 1951 and scored more than 100 runs seven times.

Inducted 1995

Dennis Eckersley, P (Red Sox 1978–1984, 1998)

Eckersley was one of a kind. He swept into Boston from Cleveland with his long black hair and neatly trimmed mustache and, not unlike Zorro, put his mark on the city. He won 20 games and lost eight in 1978 as the Red Sox and Yankees battled for supremacy. Known by many for his subsequent brilliance as a relief pitcher, the man they call Eck won 84 games as a starter before being dealt to the Cubs for Bill Buckner in 1984.

Inducted 2004

Dwight Evans, RF (Red Sox 1972–1990)

Dwight Evans was as good a right-fielder as you will ever see. He earned eight Gold Gloves roaming the vast expanses at Fenway, and many of his catches and subsequent throws back to the infield brought gasps from the fans. No runner in his right mind would challenge his powerful arm, and those foolhardy few who did soon learned not to do it again. But Evans was not a good-field, no-hit player. He also contributed 379 homers and 1,346 RBIs during his playing career, all as a member of the Sox.

Inducted 2000

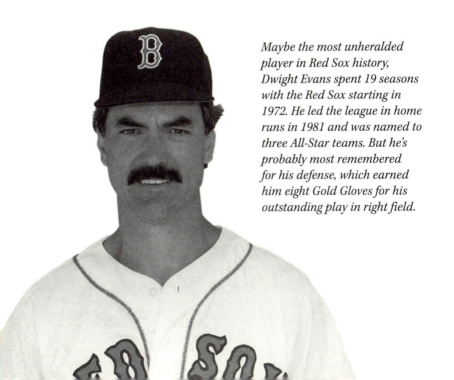

Maybe the most unheralded player in Red Sox history, Dwight Evans spent 19 seasons with the Red Sox starting in 1972. He led the league in home runs in 1981 and was named to three All-Star teams. But he's probably most remembered for his defense, which earned him eight Gold Gloves for his outstanding play in right field.

Boo Ferriss, P (Red Sox 1945–1950)

Boo Ferriss had a reputation that was impossible to escape. He was nice. If there was a hall of fame for niceness, Boo would be enshrined, everybody from Parnell to Pesky to Williams agreed on that. He was also a great pitcher. Ferriss broke in with a 21–10 rookie season mark (2.96 ERA) in 1945 and followed that up with a sophomore campaign in which he defied the jinx and went 25–6 and held the St. Louis Cardinals scoreless in a World Series start.

Inducted 2002

Carlton Fisk, C (Red Sox 1969, 1971–1980)

Fisk will always be remembered for one game and one at-bat, but his career was a long one and his overall record as a member of the Red Sox more than qualifies him for admittance to the Bosox Hall of Fame. Sox fans knew they had something special even before the Vermont native officially captured the Rookie of the Year award in 1972. He jolted 22 home runs that season and batted .293 while winning a Gold Glove at one of the most physically and mentally demanding positions in any sport. His final Boston average was .284 and he hit 162 of his major league total 376 homers as a member of the Sox, earning him a total of seven All-Star selections.

Inducted 1997

Larry Gardner, 3B (Red Sox 1908–1917)

Gardner played when the Red Sox were a powerhouse, and he was one of their early standouts. A New Englander of hearty Vermont stock, he played on three Red Sox World Series championship teams. His biggest historical achievement was securing a win for the Sox in the very first Series in 1912, as he tapped a tenth-inning Christy Mathewson offering far enough to score a run via the sac fly.

Inducted 2000

Tex Hughson, P (Red Sox 1941–1949)

Hughson's career was short, but oh so sweet. In eight seasons as a Red Sox hurler, he won 96 games and lost 54 with a highly respectable 2.94 ERA. In 1942 he went 22–6 and led the AL with 113 strikeouts. He also spearheaded the Red Sox 1946 drive to the AL pennant with a 20–11 record.

Inducted 2002

Bruce Hurst, P (Red Sox 1980–1988)

Left-handed pitchers at Fenway are about as successful as vendors of Yankees pennants and George Steinbrenner masks. Hurst was one of the few exceptions. The Mormon compiled a striking 33–9 Fenway record from '86 to '88 and won a total of 56 in the "lyric little bandbox" that seems coffin-like to many southpaws. Among lefties, only Mel Parnell

Jim Lonborg had one great year, 1967, when he won 22 games, led the league in strikeouts, won the Cy Young Award, and helped pitch the Red Sox to the 1967 pennant. He also won two games in the 1967 World Series but lost Game 7 to Bob Gibson of the St. Louis Cardinals.

has more Fenway victories. Hurst's postseason record is even more impressive. In the 1986 World Series he went 2–0 with a 1.96 ERA and was in line to win MVP honors until the earth stopped rotating on its axis. Hurst's Red Sox career record was 93–73 and perhaps the ultimate compliment was paid him by the Mets' Darryl Strawberry, who said straight-faced. "Clemens in tough, but he's no Bruce Hurst."

Inducted 2004

Jackie Jensen, RF (Red Sox 1954–1959, 1961)

Jensen had a fear of flying that shortened his career, but while a member of the Red Sox he was flying high, winning the AL MVP award in 1958. A *Sports Illustrated* cover story of that year declared him the "Workhorse of the Red Sox" and he really was. He played in 1,039 games for Boston during his short time there and led the league in stolen bases (once) and RBIs (three times). He also led Boston in RBIs six times.

Inducted 2000

Duffy Lewis, LF (Red Sox 1910–1917)

Lewis, Speaker, and Hooper made up the most potent outfield of the era. Duffy Lewis is arguably the least known of the three but he was part of a trio of championship Sox squads and had a feature of Fenway Park—a hill in front of old left-field fence—named after him because of his skill in negotiating it.

Inducted 2002

Jim Lonborg, P (Red Sox 1965–1971)

Lonborg captured the Cy Young Award in 1967 with a 22–9 record as he led the Red Sox to the American League pennant against 100–1 odds. An iron man of the mound, he pitched 15 complete games that year, led the league in strikeouts, and boasted a 3.16 ERA. In the 1967 World Series against St. Louis he won two and lost one, tossed a one-hitter, and contributed two more nine-inning starts. His career went downhill after an off-season skiing accident, and he finished with a 68–65 record as a member of the Red Sox.

Inducted 2002

Fred Lynn, OF (Red Sox 1974–1980)

Fred Lynn was a natural, a once-in-a-lifetime ballplayer with all the tools for stardom. He roamed center field with the grace of a gazelle, hit for average and power, and had speed on the bases. He reminded many fans of Joe DiMaggio, who had a similar effortless stride in the field and comfort zone at the plate. To say that Lynn broke in with a flourish would be to sell him short. He hit 21 homers, batted .331, and drove in 105 runs. He not only earned a Gold Glove for his play in center, but he won both the Rookie of the Year award and the MVP award in the same year and seemed destined for Cooperstown. Many claim that had he remained with the Red Sox, he would be in the Hall of Fame in Cooperstown today.

Inducted 2002

okie of the Year in 1975,
fielder Fred Lynn spent six
sons with the Red Sox and
s named an All-Star in
ry one of those years. He
the league in batting in
79 and won four Gold
ves as a Red Sox player.

Famous Last Words/Parting Shots

1. Ted Williams wordless home run in his last at-bat was more articulate than any spoken good-bye could be.

2. "Get the guys ready in case I get in trouble." —Red Sox pitcher Pedro Martinez, to manager Grady Little before going out to pitch the eighth inning of Game 7 of the 2003 ALCS

3. "I think it was Casey Stengel who said, 'Once you get an opportunity to manage, the only way you're not going to get fired is if you die on the bench or you're the owner of the club.'" —Grady Little, after being fired by the Red Sox

4. "We are 3–1 now. You never know what can happen, but we're going to keep playing the game." —David Ortiz after winning Game 4 of the 2004 ALCS with a walkoff two-run homer

5. "There's definitely a little sadness. I'm leaving a place I love. What we had on the field was pretty special. Off the field, I'll never forget the way the fans embraced me." —Nomar Garciaparra after being traded to the Chicago Cubs

6. "In spite of the terrible things that have been said about me by the knights of the keyboard up there...and they were terrible things...I'd like to forget them but I can't...I want to say that my years in Boston have been the greatest thing in my life." —Ted Williams addressing the Fenway Park crowd before his last major league game and taking a final shot at the writers who had made his life so miserable

7. "Who wants to be on a team that goes down in history with the '64 Phillies and the '67 Arabs?" —Bill Lee's parting shot on learning that he had been traded to the Montreal Expos after the 1978 season

8. "I feel just playing one game at Fenway Park makes me a winner. I loved the competition. I always gave my best. I might not have had the greatest ability in the

world, but I got the most out of it...I hope I represented Boston and New England with class and dignity."
—Carl Yastrzemski addressing a full house at Fenway before his last major league game. (He then did something that Ted Williams had failed do so many years earlier, by stubbornly refusing to tip his cap. He acknowledged the fans by running past the stands, tipping his hat, slapping hands, and generally making them a part of the event.)

9. "I thought you said that Bernie was like a son to you? Well, I've got news for you, you don't trade your son to Cleveland." —Bill Lee to Don Zimmer after his friend and teammate Bernie Carbo had been dealt to the Indians

10. "My heart will always be in Boston." —Babe Ruth after being sold to New York in 1920

Frank Malzone, 3B (Red Sox 1955–1965)

Frank Malzone was the Red Sox version of Brooks Robinson. He was an eight-time All-Star selection and won three Gold Gloves as a member of the Red Sox. In his rookie campaign he had 10 assists in a single game to tie the American League mark.

Inducted 1995

Bill Monbouquette, RHP (Red Sox 1958–1965)

A hometown boy from Medford, Massachusetts, the man they called Monbo was one of the aces of the Red Sox staff during the years when the franchise was struggling on the field and at the gate. Despite pitching for mediocre teams with little run support, he won 96 games, lost 91, and managed a 3.69 ERA while with the Red Sox. Each year brought a new accomplishment. In 1960 he pitched well enough to earn the right to start that year's All-Star Game. In 1961 he struck out 17 Washington Senators. In 1962 he threw a no-hitter against Chicago. He won 20 games in 1963 for a Sox team that had only 76 wins and finished seventh in the AL. He was named to the American League All-Star squad four times.

Inducted 2000

Mel Parnell, P (Red Sox 1947–1956)

Parnell was a lifer with the Red Sox, and his name is always mentioned among the elite pitchers who have toed the rubber for the Boston AL franchise. In his 10-year career, he boasts a 123–75 (.621) record and a highly respectable 3.50 ERA. In 1949, Parnell recorded a 25–7 record with a 2.77 ERA. He was a workhorse that year, completing 27 games and leading the league in most mound stats to earn a starting slot in the All-Star Game. He followed that stellar performance with back-to-back 18-win seasons and then went 21–8 in 1953, lowering his ERA to 3.06. In 1956 he pitched a no-hitter against the Chicago White Sox at Fenway Park. His 123 wins are the most ever by a Red Sox southpaw.

Inducted 1997

Johnny Pesky, SS-3B (Red Sox 1942, 1946–1952)

During an incredible playing and coaching career, Johnny Pesky has earned the title Mr. Red Sox. His accomplishments on the field are impressive, and he was a part of the great foursome of loyal teammates who hailed from the West Coast. The others were Ted Williams, Bobby Doerr, and Dom DiMaggio.

It took 55 years for someone to break his rookie record of 205 base hits by a Red Sox player. And it took a superstar like Nomar Garciaparra (209 in 1997) to accomplish the feat.

With a lifetime Boston average of .313, Pesky ranks in the top 10, and when you consider how many batting champions played in Boston the feat becomes even more impressive. He recorded three consecutive 200-hit seasons, leading the league each time. Hitters such as Pesky and DiMaggio set the table for Ted Williams and other Red Sox sluggers. Pesky played that role as well as anyone, past or present.

Inducted 1995

Rico Petrocelli, SS-3B (Red Sox 1963, 1965–1976)

At a time when infielders were supposed to be good-field, no-hit performers, Rico Petrocelli changed that notion. In 1969 he hit a record 40 homers while playing shortstop. In all, he powered 210 home runs for the Red Sox. He was no slouch in the field either, and was twice selected to start at shortstop for the AL All-Star team. Rico was a standout in the

1967 World Series against St. Louis. He homered twice in Game 6. He also performed well in the 1975 Fall Classic, batting .308 against the Big Red Machine.
Inducted 1997

Dick Radatz, P (Red Sox 1962–1966)

The impact of Dick Radatz is difficult to underestimate. He was a phenomenon. When he entered the game, he was in complete control, and the sight of this 6'6" "Monster" staring in from the mound must have been disconcerting to enemy batters. Radatz was a true Yankees killer, performing at his best against the best team in baseball. Twice named AL Fireman of the Year, Radatz saved a total of 104 games for some very weak Red Sox teams. He arrived on the scene in 1962 and promptly led the league in saves with 24 and relief wins with 9. Anyone who witnessed his dominance in the 1963 All-Star Game will not soon forget it. He struck out Willie Mays, Dick Groat, Duke Snider, Willie McCovey, and Julian Javier in just two innings of work.
Inducted 1997

Jim Rice, OF (Red Sox 1974–1989)

Jim Rice was known as the Boston Strongman. And with good reason. Stories of him breaking bats on checked swings and hitting baseballs out of sight are part of Red Sox lore. He was one of those players feared by pitchers throughout baseball because of his grooved swing. He was also one of those players who faded quickly when the end came. He finished his career with 382 homers and 2,452 hits. Rice had a great year in helping to lead the Red Sox to the 1975 World Series. He batted .309 with 22 home runs and 102 RBIs in his rookie campaign before being sidelined by injury for the postseason. Red Sox fans still wonder what might have happened had a healthy Rice been in the lineup. He won MVP honors in 1978, beating out Yankees pitcher Ron Guidry in a close race. That year Rice accomplished two-thirds of baseball's Triple Crown, leading the AL with 46 homers

TRIVIA

What was the Opening Day lineup for the very first Boston American League franchise?

Answers to the trivia questions are on pages 175–176.

and 139 RBIs. He also led in hits with 213 and in triples with 15. His batting average of .315 wasn't too shabby either, third-best in the league behind only Rod Carew (.333) and Al Oliver (.324). Perhaps his major accomplishment that year was passing 400 total bases, the first right-handed hitter to do so since Joe DiMaggio some 40 years earlier. During 11 different seasons, he hit at least 20 homers! Rice was an All-Star eight times during his 16-year reign as the Boston Strongman.

Inducted on 1995

Pete Runnels, IF (Red Sox 1958–1962)

Pete Runnels was not Ted Williams, but he did win two American League batting titles—in 1960 with a .320 mark and in 1962 with .326—and finished just percentage points behind Ted in 1958. Another of the parade of great left-handed hitters who have thrived at Fenway, Runnels never hit below .300 in any of his five seasons in Boston.

Inducted 2004

Reggie Smith, CF (Red Sox 1966–1973)

Reggie Smith's first full season in Boston in 1967 coincided with the Red Sox revival as a competitive franchise. Smith was a switch-hitting out-fielder with power who played centerfield between Carl Yastrzemski in left and Tony Conigliaro in right. The *Sporting News* called them the "best outfield in baseball." Smith could do it all, as evidenced by his two All-Star Game selections while with the Red Sox. At the plate he batted over .300 three times for the Sox and twice led the league in doubles. He also chipped in with a Gold Glove in 1968. He came through in the clutch, hitting two homers in the '67 World Series against the St. Louis Cardinals. He hit 149 homers while with Boston and batted .281 with 536 RBIs.

Inducted 2000

Bob Stanley, P (Red Sox 1977–1989)

Stanley is another of those players whose accomplishments are often overlooked due to events in a single key game. Stanley came into Game 6 of the 1986 World Series to replace reliever Calvin Schiraldi. With two outs, the Red Sox were one out away from the World Championship. His

ALL-TIME Red Sox Team

Postion	Player
1B	Jimmie Foxx
2B	Bobby Doerr
3B	Wade Boggs
SS	Nomar Garciaparra
C	Carlton Fisk
OF	Ted Williams
OF	Carl Yastrzemski
OF	Tris Speaker
DH	David Ortiz
RHPs	Roger Clemens, Pedro Martinez, Cy Young
LHPs	Lefty Grove, Mel Parnell
Reliever	Dick Radatz
Manager	Dick Williams

inside pitch to Mookie Wilson escaped catcher Rich Gedman, allowing the tying run to score from third. Stanley then induced an innocent little ground ball to Bill Buckner that eluded him, and the Sox went on to lose the game and Series.

The Maine native known as the "Steamer" nevertheless had a fine career in Boston, posting a 115–97 record in 637 appearances on the mound, a record 85 of those wins coming in relief. Sporting a 3.64 ERA, the two-time All-Star saved a record 132 games for the Red Sox. Stanley's signature season was 1978, when he went 15–2, 13 of those victories coming in relief. He led the American League in relief wins in 1981 with 10. In 1983 he established what was then the team mark for saves with 33.

Inducted 2000

Luis Tiant, P (Red Sox 1971–1978)

Luis Tiant was one of the most popular Red Sox players of all time. He won 20 games three times while with the Red Sox and was an integral part of the great Red Sox teams of the '70s.

Inducted 1997

Smoky Joe Wood, P (Red Sox 1908–1915)

Who can say what Joe Wood might have accomplished if not for an injury that curtailed his pitching career?

Smoky Joe threw the ball faster than any man alive, according to no less an authority than Walter "Big Train" Johnson. Smoky Joe had a Red Sox ERA of 1.99 while winning 117 games and losing only 56. In 1911 he spun a no-hitter against the St. Louis Browns. In 1912 he led the Boston AL franchise to the World Series title, winning a Red Sox record 34 games against only 5 losses. Many claim that this is the best single-season pitching record of the century, and it would be difficult to refute the claim. He also had 258 strikeouts and his ERA was 1.91 that year. Once in the Series, he won three more games to clinch the title. Wood's last year in Boston was arguably his strongest. He went 15–5 and crafted a 1.49 ERA.

Inducted 1995

ANSWERS TO TRIVIA QUESTIONS

Page 2: Jimmy Collins

Page 2: Baltimore. On April 26, 1901, they played their first American League game in Baltimore and lost 10–6.

Page 3: Cy Young. On May 8, 1901, he posted the first home win for Boston. The score was 12–4.

Page 4: The Huntington Avenue Grounds

Page 11: From 1912 to 1934, Fenway's left field featured a 10-foot-high incline known as "Duffy's Cliff." It was so named because of left fielder Duffy Lewis' ability to navigate it so expertly. It was flattened for the 1935 season by order of owner Tom Yawkey, and some 70 years later, Manny Ramirez and all of Red Sox Nation are grateful to Yawkey for preventing untold disasters.

Page 12: He had no uniform number while he played in Boston. Major league baseball players did not start wearing uniform numbers until 1929, when Ruth was in New York. The Babe was issued No. 3 that year because he batted third in the Yankees lineup.

Page 14: The *Titanic* hitting the iceberg was bigger news than the Red Sox hitting their new field.

Page 15: It was located in an area of Boston known locally as "the Fens."

Page 17: 25 (Ted Williams did it 6 times; Wade Boggs, 5; Carl Yastrzemski, 3; Pete Runnels and Nomar Garciaparra, 2 times each; and 1 each by Dale Alexander, Jimmie Foxx, Billy Goodman, Fred Lynn, Carney Lansford, Manny Ramirez, and Bill Mueller)

Page 21: 37 feet

Page 22 Cy Young and Roger Clemens

Page 25: c) Jimmie Foxx, with 50 in 1938

Page 35: Joe Gordon (1942) and Joe DiMaggio (1947)

Page 37: Ted Williams, Jimmy Piersall, and Jackie Jensen

Page 41: The Boudreau Shift (sometimes called the "Williams Shift") was a dramatic defensive positioning that attempted to foil the pull-hitting Ted Williams. The entire infield and outfield were moved toward the right side of the ball field. It was introduced in 1946 by Cleveland Indians player-manager Lou Boudreau. Despite the shift, Williams managed to bat .342 that year, with 38 home runs and 123 RBIs.

Page 47: "Playing the Field"

Page 55: Taters

Page 76: Luis Tiant pitched a five-hit shutout against the Cincinnati Reds in a 6–0 win in Game 1 (he also chipped in with a single and scored the game's first run). He was touched for four runs in Game 4, but stayed in to complete the game and notched his second victory. He also started Game 6 for the Bosox, but was lifted after giving up six runs in seven innings. Although he got a no-decision, Boston went on to win the game in the twelfth inning on a Carlton Fisk walk-off home run. Tiant was the starter in all three of the games that the Sox won in the 1975 World Series, pitching a total of 25 innings.

Page 78: Fred Lynn

Page 91: Jim Rice played in 163 games in 1978, including the infamous one-game playoff with the Yankees, also known as "the Bucky Dent Game."

Page 101: 24. On June 23, 1982, Wade Boggs, a rookie fresh from Pawtucket, powered his first career home run. It came in dramatic fashion in the bottom of the eleventh inning against the Detroit Tigers and gave the Red Sox a 5–4 win. When regular third baseman Carney Lansford sprained his ankle the very next day, Boggs moved into the lineup and eventually into the Hall of Fame.

Page 102: Two, both as a member of the New York Yankees

Page 109: Nomar Garciaparra

Page 111: b) Johnny Damon

Page 111: Edgar Renteria

Page 112: Trot Nixon on July 15, 2005, in a 17–1 drubbing of the New York Yankees. "Thank goodness there wasn't a throw [home]," said a tired Nixon afterward. "I'd've had to probably crawl up there to the plate, where Posada was." He added that he needed "an oxygen mask."

Page 143: Johnny Damon

Page 144: David Wells

Page 171:
1. LF—Tommy Dowd
2. RF—Charles Hemphill
3. CF—Chick Stahl
4. 3B—Jimmy Collins
5. 1B—Buck Freeman
6. SS—Fred Parent
7. 2B—Hobe Ferris
8. C—Lou Criger
9. P—Win Kellum

*Note: Larry McLean was inserted as a pinch-hitter.

Boston Red Sox All-Time Roster

Players who have appeared in at least one game with the Red Sox

* Player still active in Major League Baseball

A

Luis Aparicio (SS)	1971–73
Luis Aponte (P)	1980–83
Pete Appleton (P)	1932
Frank Arellanes (P)	1908–10
Tony Armas (OF)	1983–86
Charlie Armbruster (C)	1905–07
Rolando Arrojo (P)	2001–02
Bronson Arroyo* (P)	2004–05
Casper Asbjornson (C)	1928–29
Billy Ashley (OF)	1998
Ken Aspromonte (2B)	1957–58
Pedro Astacio* (P)	2004
James Atkins (P)	1950, 1952
Elden Auker (P)	1939
Leslie Aulds (C)	1947
Steve Avery (P)	1997–98
Bobby Avila (2B)	1959
Ramon Aviles (2B)	1977
Joe Azcue (C)	1969

B

Lore Bader (P)	1917–18
Carlos Baerga* (2B)	2002
Jim Bagby (P)	1938–40, 1946
Bob Bailey (3B)	1977–78
Cory Bailey (P)	1993–94
Gene Bailey (OF)	1920
Jeff Bailey* (C)	2004–05
Al Baker (P)	1938
Floyd Baker (3B)	1953–54
Jack Baker (1B)	1976–77
Tracy Baker (1B)	1911
Neal Ball (SS)	1912–13
Scott Bankhead (P)	1993–94
Willie Banks* (P)	2002
Travis Baptist (P)	1999
Walter Barbare (3B)	1918
Frank Barberich (P)	1910
Brian Bark (P)	1995
Brian Barkley (P)	1998
Babe Barna (OF)	1943
Steve Barr (P)	1974–75
Bill Barrett (OF)	1929–30
Bob Barrett (3B)	1929
Frank Barrett (P)	1944–45
Jimmy Barrett (OF)	1907–08
Marty Barrett (2B)	1982–90
Tom Barrett (2B)	1992
Ed Barry (P)	1905–07
Jack Barry (SS)	1915–17, 1919
Matt Batts (C)	1947–51
Frank Baumann (P)	1955–59
Tim Bausher* (P)	2004–05
Don Baylor (DH)	1986–87
Bill Bayne (P)	1929–30
Rod Beck* (P)	2001

Hugh Bedient (P)	1912–14
Matt Beech* (P)	2004
Stan Belinda (P)	1995–96
Gary Bell (P)	1967–68
Juan Bell (2B)	1995
Mark Bellhorn* (2B)	2004–05
Esteban Beltre (SS)	1996
Juan Beniquez (OF)	1971–72, 1974–75
Mike Benjamin* (SS)	1997–98
Dennis Bennett (P)	1965–67
Frank Bennett (P)	1927–28
Al Benton (P)	1952
Todd Benzinger (1B)	1987–88
Lou Berberet (C)	1958
Dave Berg* (2B)	2005
Moe Berg (C)	1935–39
Boze Berger (2B)	1939
Charlie Berry (C)	1928–32
Sean Berry* (3B)	2000
Damon Berryhill (C)	1994
Hal Bevan (3B)	1952
Ben Beville (P)	1901
Dante Bichette (OF)	2000–01
Elliot Bigelow (OF)	1929
Jack Billingham (P)	1980
Doug Bird (P)	1983
John Bischoff (C)	1925–26
Max Bishop (2B)	1934–35
Dave Black (P)	1923
Tim Blackwell (C)	1974–75
Clarence Blethen (P)	1923
Greg Blosser (OF)	1993–94
Red Bluhm (—)	1918
Mike Boddicker (P)	1988–90
Larry Boerner (P)	1932
Wade Boggs (3B)	1982–92
Bobby Bolin (P)	1970–73
Milt Bolling (SS)	1952–57
Tom Bolton (P)	1987–92
Ike Boone (OF)	1923–25
Ray Boone (3B)	1960
Toby Borland* (P)	1997

Tom Borland (P)	1960–61
Lou Boudreau (SS)	1951–52
Sam Bowen (OF)	1977–78, 1980
Stew Bowers (P)	1935–37
Joe Bowman (P)	1944–45
Ted Bowsfield (P)	1958–60
Oil Can Boyd (P)	1982–89
Chad Bradford* (P)	2005
Herb Bradley (P)	1927–29
Hugh Bradley (1B)	1910–12
King Brady (P)	1908
Cliff Brady (2B)	1920
Darren Bragg* (OF)	1996–98
Mark Brandenburg (P)	1996–97
Bucky Brandon (P)	1966–68
Fred Bratschi (OF)	1926–27
Eddie Bressoud (SS)	1962–65
Ken Brett (P)	1967, 1969–71
Tom Brewer (P)	1954–61
Ralph Brickner (P)	1952
Jim Brillheart (P)	1931
Dick Brodowski (P)	1952, 1955
Rico Brogna (1B)	2000
Jack Brohamer (2B)	1978–80
Adrian Brown* (CF)	2003
Hal Brown (P)	1953–55
Jamie Brown* (P)	2004
Kevin Brown (C)	2002
Lloyd Brown (P)	1933
Mace Brown (P)	1942–43, 1946
Mike Brown (P)	1982–86
Mike Brumley (SS)	1991–92
Tom Brunansky (OF)	1990–92, 1994
Jim Bucher (3B)	1944–45
Bill Buckner (1B)	1984–87, 1990
Don Buddin (SS)	1956, 1958–61
Damon Buford (OF)	1998–99
Kirk Bullinger* (P)	1999
Fred Burchell (P)	1907–09
Bob Burda (1B)	1972
Tom Burgmeier (P)	1978–82
Jesse Burkett (OF)	1905

John Burkett (P)	2002–03
Morgan Burkhart* (1B)	2000–01
Ellis Burks (OF)	1987–92, 2004
Rick Burleson (SS)	1974–80
George Burns (1B)	1922–23
Jim Burton (P)	1975, 1977
Jim Busby (OF)	1959–60
Joe Bush (P)	1918–21
Jack Bushelman (P)	1911–12
Frank Bushey (P)	1927, 1930
Bill Butland (P)	1940, 1942, 1946–47
Bud Byerly (P)	1958
Jim Byrd (—)	1993

C

Orlando Cabrera* (SS)	2004
Hick Cady (C)	1912–17
Ivan Calderon (OF)	1993
Earl Caldwell (P)	1948
Ray Caldwell (P)	1919
Dolph Camilli (1B)	1945
Bill Campbell (P)	1977–81
Paul Campbell (1B)	1941–42, 1946
Jose Canseco (OF)	1995–96
Bernie Carbo (OF)	1974–78
Tom Carey (2B)	1939–42, 1946
Walter Carlisle (OF)	1908
Swede Carlstrom (SS)	1911
Cleo Carlyle (OF)	1927
Roy Carlyle (OF)	1925–26
Hector Carrasco* (P)	2000
Bill Carrigan (C)	1906, 1908–16
Ed Carroll (P)	1929
Jerry Casale (P)	1958–60
Joe Cascarella (P)	1935–36
Scott Cassidy* (P)	2005
Carlos Castillo* (P)	2001
Frank Castillo* (P)	2001–02
Danny Cater (1B)	1972–74
Rex Cecil (P)	1944–45
Orlando Cepeda (1B)	1973
Rick Cerone (C)	1988–89

Chet Chadbourne (OF)	1906–07
Bob Chakales (P)	1957
Wes Chamberlain (OF)	1994–95
Esty Chaney (P)	1913
Ed Chaplin (C)	1920–22
Ben Chapman (OF)	1937–38
Pete Charton (P)	1964
Ken Chase (P)	1942–43
Charlie Chech (P)	1909
Robinson Checo (P)	1997–98
Bruce Chen* (P)	2003
Jack Chesbro (P)	1909
Nelson Chittum (P)	1959–60
Jin Ho Cho* (P)	1998–99
Joe Christopher (OF)	1966
Loyd Christopher (OF)	1945
Joe Cicero (OF)	1929–30
Eddie Cicotte (P)	1908–12
Galen Cisco (P)	1961–62, 1967
Bill Cissell (2B)	1934
Danny Clark (3B)	1924
Jack Clark (OF)	1991–92
Otie Clark (P)	1945
Phil Clark (OF)	1996
Tony Clark* (1B)	2002
Mark Clear (P)	1981–85
Roger Clemens* (P)	1984–96
Matt Clement* (P)	2005
Lance Clemons (P)	1974
Reggie Cleveland (P)	1974–78
Tex Clevenger (P)	1954
Lou Clinton (OF)	1960–64
Bill Clowers (P)	1926
George Cochran (3B)	1918
Jack Coffey (SS)	1918
Alex Cole (OF)	1996
Dave Coleman (OF)	1977
Michael Coleman* (DH)	1997, 1999
Lou Collier* (SS)	2003
Jimmy Collins (3B)	1901–07
Ray Collins (P)	1909–15
Rip Collins (P)	1922

Shano Collins (OF)	1921–25
Merl Combs (SS)	1947, 1949–50
Ralph Comstock (P)	1915
David Cone (P)	2001
Bunk Congalton (OF)	1907
Billy Conigliaro (OF)	1969–71
Tony Conigliaro (OF)	1964–67, 1969–70, 1975
Gene Conley (P)	1961–63
Bud Connolly (SS)	1925
Ed Connolly (C)	1929–32
Ed Connolly (P)	1964
Joe Connolly (OF)	1924
Bill Conroy (C)	1942–44
Billy Consolo (SS)	1953–59
Dusty Cooke (OF)	1933–36
Jimmy Cooney (SS)	1917
Cecil Cooper (1B)	1971–76
Guy Cooper (P)	1914–15
Scott Cooper (3B)	1990–94
Alex Cora* (2B)	2005
Wil Cordero* (1B)	1996–97
Rheal Cormier* (P)	1995, 1999–00
Vic Correll (C)	1972
Jim Corsi (P)	1997–99
Marlan Coughtry (2B)	1960
Fritz Coumbe (P)	1914
Ted Cox (3B)	1977
Doc Cramer (OF)	1936–40
Gavvy Cravath (OF)	1908
Paxton Crawford* (P)	2000–01
Steve Crawford (P)	1980–82, 1984–87
Pat Creeden (2B)	1931
Bob Cremins (P)	1927
Cesar Crespo* (2B)	2004
Jack Cressend* (P)	2005
Lou Criger (C)	1901–08
Joe Cronin (SS)	1935–45
Zach Crouch (P)	1988
Rick Croushore* (P)	2000–01
Jose Cruz* (CF)	2005
Leon Culberson (OF)	1943–47
Ray Culp (P)	1968–73

Chris Cumberland (—)	1999
Midre Cummings* (OF)	1998, 2000
Nig Cuppy (P)	1901
Steve Curry (P)	1988
John Curtis (P)	1970–73
Milt Cuyler (OF)	1996

D

Babe Dahlgren (1B)	1935–36
Pete Daley (C)	1955–59
Dom Dallessandro (OF)	1937
Johnny Damon* (OF)	2002–05
Babe Danzig (1B)	1909
Bobby Darwin (OF)	1976–77
Danny Darwin (P)	1991–94
Brian Daubach* (1B)	1999–02, 2004
Bob Daughters (—)	1937
Andre Dawson (OF)	1993–94
Cot Deal (P)	1947–48
Rob Deer (OF)	1993
Pep Deininger (OF)	1902
Manny Delcarmen* (P)	2005
Alex Delgado* (C)	1996
Ike Delock (P)	1952–53, 1955–63
Don Demeter (OF)	1966–67
Brian Denman (P)	1982
Sam Dente (SS)	1947
Mike Derrick (OF)	1970
Gene Desautels (C)	1937–40
Marc Deschenes* (P)	2004
Mel Deutsch (P)	1946
Mickey Devine (C)	1920
Hal Deviney (P)	1920
Al Devormer (C)	1923
Lenny DiNardo* (P)	2004
Gary DiSarcina (SS)	2002
Bo Diaz (C)	1977
Juan Diaz* (1B)	2002
George Dickey (C)	1935–36
Emerson Dickman (P)	1936, 1938–41
Bob Didier (C)	1974
Steve Dillard (2B)	1975–77

Dom DiMaggio (OF)	1940–42, 1946–53
Bill Dinneen (P)	1902–07
Bob Dipietro (OF)	1951
Ray Dobens (P)	1929
Joe Dobson (P)	1941–43, 1946–50, 1954
Sam Dodge (P)	1921–22
Pat Dodson (1B)	1986–88
Bobby Doerr (2B)	1937–44, 1946–51
John Doherty (P)	1996
Andy Dominique* (C)	2004
John Donahue (OF)	1923
Pat Donahue (C)	1908–10
Chris Donnels* (3B)	1995
Pete Donohue (P)	1932
John Dopson (P)	1989–93
Tom Doran (C)	1904–06
Harry Dorish (P)	1947–49, 1956
Jim Dorsey (P)	1984–85
Patsy Dougherty (OF)	1902–04
Tommy Dowd (OF)	1901
Danny Doyle (C)	1943
Denny Doyle (2B)	1975–77
Dick Drago (P)	1974–75, 1978–80
Clem Dreisewerd (P)	1944–46
Walt Dropo (1B)	1949–52
Jean Dubuc (P)	1918
Matt Duff* (P)	2004
Frank Duffy (SS)	1978–79
Joe Dugan (3B)	1922
Bob Duliba (P)	1965
George Dumont (P)	1919
Ed Durham (P)	1929–32
Cedric Durst (OF)	1930
Jim Dwyer (OF)	1979–80

E

Arnold Earley (P)	1960–65
Mike Easler (OF)	1984–85
Dennis Eckersley (P)	1978–84, 1998
Elmer Eggert (2B)	1927
Howard Ehmke (P)	1923–26
Hack Eibel (OF)	1920

Dick Ellsworth (P)	1968–69
Steve Ellsworth (P)	1988
Alan Embree* (P)	2003–05
Clyde Engle (OF)	1910–14
Todd Erdos* (P)	2001
Nick Esasky (1B)	1989
Vaughn Eshelman (P)	1995–97
Al Evans (C)	1951
Bill Evans (P)	1951
Dwight Evans (OF)	1972–90
Carl Everett* (OF)	2000–01
Hoot Evers (OF)	1952–54
Homer Ezzell (3B)	1924–25

F

Carmen Fanzone (3B)	1970
Steve Farr (P)	1994
Doc Farrell (SS)	1935
Duke Farrell (C)	1903–05
Jeff Fassero* (P)	2000
Alex Ferguson (P)	1922–25
Rick Ferrell (C)	1933–37
Wes Ferrell (P)	1934–37
Hobe Ferris (2B)	1901–07
Dave Ferriss (P)	1945–50
Chick Fewster (2B)	1922–23
Joel Finch (P)	1979
Tommy Fine (P)	1947
Lou Finney (OF)	1939–42, 1944–45
Gar Finnvold (P)	1994
Mike Fiore (1B)	1970–71
Hank Fischer (P)	1966–67
Carlton Fisk (C)	1969, 1971–80
Howie Fitzgerald (OF)	1926
Ira Flagstead (OF)	1923–29
John Flaherty* (C)	1992–93
Al Flair (1B)	1941
Bill Fleming (P)	1940–41
Scott Fletcher (SS)	1993–94
Bryce Florie* (P)	2000–01
Ben Flowers (P)	1951, 1953
Cliff Floyd* (OF)	2002

Chad Fonville (2B)	1999	Nomar Garciaparra* (SS)	1996–04
Frank Foreman (P)	1901	Mike Gardiner (P)	1991–92
Happy Foreman (P)	1926	Billy Gardner (2B)	1962–63
Mike Fornieles (P)	1957–63	Larry Gardner (3B)	1908–17
Gary Fortune (P)	1920	Wes Gardner (P)	1986–90
Casey Fossum* (P)	2002–03	Mike Garman (P)	1969, 1971–73
Eddie Foster (3B)	1920–22	Cliff Garrison (P)	1928
Rube Foster (P)	1913–17	Ford Garrison (OF)	1943–44
Bob Fothergill (OF)	1933	Alex Gaston (C)	1926, 1929
Keith Foulke* (P)	2004–05	Milt Gaston (P)	1929–31
Boob Fowler (SS)	1926	Rich Gedman (C)	1980–90
Chad Fox* (P)	2003	Gary Geiger (OF)	1959–65
Pete Fox (OF)	1941–45	Charlie Gelbert (SS)	1940
Jimmie Foxx (1B)	1936–42	Wally Gerber (SS)	1928–29
Joe Foy (3B)	1966–68	Dick Gernert (1B)	1952–59
Ray Francis (P)	1925	Doc Gessler (OF)	1908–09
Buck Freeman (OF)	1901–07	Chappie Geygan (SS)	1924–26
Hersh Freeman (P)	1952–53, 1955	Jeremy Giambi* (LF)	2003
John Freeman (OF)	1927	Joe Giannini (SS)	1911
Charlie French (2B)	1909–10	Norwood Gibson (P)	1903–06
Bernie Friberg (3B)	1933	Russ Gibson (C)	1967–69
Owen Friend (2B)	1955	Andy Gilbert (OF)	1942, 1946
Todd Frohwirth (P)	1994	Don Gile (1B)	1959–62
Jeff Frye (2B)	1996–97, 1999–00	Frank Gilhooley (OF)	1919
Oscar Fuhr (P)	1924–25	Bernard Gilkey (OF)	2000
Frank Fuller (2B)	1923	Bob Gillespie (P)	1950
Curt Fullerton (P)	1921–25, 1933	Grant Gillis (2B)	1929
		Joe Ginsberg (C)	1961
G		Ralph Glaze (P)	1906–08
Gary Gaetti (3B)	2000	Harry Gleason (3B)	1901–03
Fabian Gaffke (OF)	1936–39	Joe Glenn (C)	1940
Phil Gagliano (2B)	1971–72	John Godwin (3B)	1905–06
Del Gainer (1B)	1914–17, 1919	Chuck Goggin (2B)	1974
Rich Gale (P)	1984	Wayne Gomes* (P)	2002
Denny Galehouse (P)	1939–40, 1947–49	Joe Gonzales (P)	1937
Bob Gallagher (OF)	1972	Eusebio Gonzalez (SS)	1918
Ed Gallagher (P)	1932	Jeremi Gonzalez* (P)	2005
Jim Galvin (—)	1930	Johnny Gooch (C)	1933
Bob Garbark (C)	1945	Billy Goodman (2B)	1947–57
Rich Garces* (P)	1996–01	Tom Gordon* (P)	1996–99
Freddy Garcia* (3B)	2000	Jim Gosger (OF)	1963, 1965–66
Reynaldo Garcia* (P)	2004	Tony Graffanino* (2B)	2005

Charlie Graham (C)	1906
Lee Graham (OF)	1983
Skinny Graham (OF)	1934–35
Dave Gray (P)	1964
Jeff Gray (P)	1990–91
Craig Grebeck* (2B)	2001
Lenny Green (OF)	1965–66
Pumpsie Green (2B)	1959–62
Mike Greenwell (OF)	1985–96
Vean Gregg (P)	1914–16
Doug Griffin (2B)	1971–77
Marty Griffin (P)	1928
Guido Grilli (P)	1966
Ray Grimes (1B)	1920
Myron Grimshaw (1B)	1905–07
Marv Grissom (P)	1953
Kip Gross (P)	1998–00
Turkey Gross (SS)	1925
Lefty Grove (P)	1934–41
Ken Grundt (P)	1996–97
Creighton Gubanich (C)	1999
Mike Guerra (C)	1951
Mario Guerrero (SS)	1973–74
Bobby Guindon (1B)	1964
Randy Gumpert (P)	1952
Eric Gunderson (P)	1995–96
Hy Gunning (1B)	1911
Mark Guthrie* (P)	1999
Jackie Gutierrez (SS)	1983–85
Ricky Gutierrez* (3B)	2004
Don Gutteridge (2B)	1946–47

H

Casey Hageman (P)	1911–12
John Halama* (P)	2005
Odell Hale (2B)	1941
Ray Haley (C)	1915–16
Charley Hall (P)	1909–13
Bob Hamelin (DH)	1998–99
Chris Hammond* (P)	1997
Garry Hancock (OF)	1978, 1980–82
Josh Hancock* (P)	2002

Chris Haney (P)	2002
Fred Haney (3B)	1926–27
Craig Hansen* (P)	2005
Erik Hanson (P)	1995
Carroll Hardy (OF)	1960–62
Tim Harikkala* (P)	1999
Harry Harper (P)	1920
Tommy Harper (OF)	1972–74
Billy Harrell (SS)	1961
Ken Harrelson (1B)	1967–69
Bill Harris (P)	1938
Greg Harris (P)	1989–94
Joe Harris (P)	1905–07
Joe Harris (1B)	1922–25
Mickey Harris (P)	1940–41, 1946–49
Reggie Harris* (P)	1996
Slim Harriss (P)	1926–28
Jack Harshman (P)	1959
Chuck Hartenstein (P)	1970
Grover Hartley (C)	1927
Mike Hartley (P)	1995
Charlie Hartman (P)	1908
Chad Harville* (P)	2005
Bill Haselman (C)	1995–97, 2003
Herb Hash (P)	1940–41
Andy Hassler (P)	1978–79
Billy Hatcher (OF)	1992–94
Fred Hatfield (3B)	1950–52
Scott Hatteberg* (1B)	1995–01
Grady Hatton (3B)	1954–56
Clem Hausmann (P)	1944–45
Jack Hayden (OF)	1906
Frankie Hayes (C)	1947
Ed Hearn (SS)	1910
Bryan Hebson* (P)	2003–04
Danny Heep (OF)	1989–90
Bob Heffner (P)	1963–65
Randy Heflin (P)	1945–46
Fred Heimach (P)	1926
Bob Heise (SS)	1975–76
Tommy Helms (2B)	1977
Charlie Hemphill (OF)	1901

Dave Henderson (OF)	1986–87
Rickey Henderson (OF)	2002
Tim Hendryx (OF)	1920–21
Olaf Henriksen (OF)	1911–17
Bill Henry (P)	1952–55
Butch Henry* (P)	1997–98
Jim Henry (P)	1936–37
Dustin Hermanson* (P)	2002
Ramon Hernandez (P)	1977
Mike Herrera (2B)	1925–26
Tom Herrin (P)	1954
Joe Hesketh (P)	1990–94
Eric Hetzel (P)	1989–90
Joe Heving (P)	1938–40
Johnnie Heving (C)	1924–25, 1928–30
Charlie Hickman (1B)	1902
Pinky Higgins (3B)	1937–38, 1946
Shea Hillenbrand* (3B)	2001–03
Hob Hiller (3B)	1920–21
Dave Hillman (P)	1960–61
Gordie Hinkle (C)	1934
Paul Hinrichs (P)	1951
Paul Hinson (—)	1928
Harley Hisner (P)	1951
Billy Hitchcock (3B)	1948–49
Dick Hoblitzel (1B)	1914–18
Butch Hobson (3B)	1975–80
George Hockette (P)	1934–35
Johnny Hodapp (2B)	1933
Mel Hoderlein (2B)	1951
Billy Hoeft (P)	1959
Jack Hoey (OF)	1906–08
Fred Hofmann (C)	1927–28
Glenn Hoffman (SS)	1980–87
Ken Holcombe (P)	1953
Dave Hollins (3B)	1995
Billy Holm (C)	1945
Harry Hooper (OF)	1909–
Sam Horn (DH)	1987–89
Tony Horton (1B)	1964–67
Dwayne Hosey (OF)	1995–96
Tom House (P)	1976–77

Wayne Housie (OF)	1991
Chris Howard (P)	1994
Elston Howard (C)	1967–68
Paul Howard (OF)	1909
Les Howe (P)	1923–24
Bob Howry* (P)	2002–03
Peter Hoy (P)	1992
Waite Hoyt (P)	1919–
Joe Hudson (P)	1995–97
Sid Hudson (P)	1952–54
Ed Hughes (P)	1905–06
Terry Hughes (3B)	1974
Tom Hughes (P)	1902–03
Tex Hughson (P)	1941–44, 1946–49
Tim Hummel* (3B)	2005
Bill Humphrey (P)	1938
Ben Hunt (P)	1910
Buddy Hunter (2B)	1971, 1973, 1975
Herb Hunter (3B)	1920
Tom Hurd (P)	1954–56
Bruce Hurst (P)	1980–88
Butch Huskey* (OF)	1999
Bert Husting (P)	1902
Adam Hyzdu* (OF)	2004–05

I

Daryl Irvine (P)	1990–92

J

Damian Jackson* (2B)	2003
Ron Jackson (1B)	1960
Beany Jacobson (P)	1907
Baby Doll Jacobson (OF)	1926–27
Lefty Jamerson (P)	1924
Bill James (P)	1919
Chris James (OF)	1995
Hal Janvrin (SS)	1911, 1913–17
Ray Jarvis (P)	1969–70
Reggie Jefferson (DH)	1995–99
Fergie Jenkins (P)	1976–77
Tom Jenkins (OF)	1925–26
Jackie Jensen (OF)	1954–59, 1961

Marcus Jensen (C)	2001
Keith Johns (2B)	1998
Bob Johnson (OF)	1944–45
Deron Johnson (1B)	1974–76
Earl Johnson (P)	1940–41, 1946–50
Hank Johnson (P)	1933–35
John Henry Johnson (P)	1983–84
Rankin Johnson (P)	1914
Roy Johnson (OF)	1932–35
Vic Johnson (P)	1944–45
Joel Johnston (P)	1995
Smead Jolley (OF)	1932–33
Bobby M. Jones* (P)	2004
Charlie Jones (OF)	1901
Dalton Jones (2B)	1964–69
Jake Jones (1B)	1947–48
Rick Jones (P)	1976
Sam Jones (P)	1916–21
Todd Jones* (P)	2003
Eddie Joost (SS)	1955
Duane Josephson (C)	1971–72
Oscar Judd (P)	1941–45
Joe Judge (1B)	1933–34
Ed Jurak (SS)	1982–85

K

Josh Kalinowski* (P)	2004
Rudy Kallio (P)	1925
Gabe Kapler* (DH)	2003–05
Ed Karger (P)	1909–11
Andy Karl (P)	1943
Marty Karow (SS)	1927
Ryan Karp (P)	1998–99
Benn Karr (P)	1920–22
Eddie Kasko (SS)	1966
George Kell (3B)	1952–54
Al Kellett (P)	1924
Red Kellett (SS)	1934
Win Kellum (P)	1901
Ed Kelly (P)	1914
Ken Keltner (3B)	1950
Russ Kemmerer (P)	1954–55, 1957

Fred Kendall (C)	1978
Bill Kennedy (P)	1953
John Kennedy (3B)	1970–74
Marty Keough (OF)	1956–60
Dana Kiecker (P)	1990–91
Joe Kiefer (P)	1925–26
Leo Kiely (P)	1951, 1954–56, 1958–59
Jack Killilay (P)	1911
Sunny Kim* (P)	2001
Byung-Hyun Kim* (P)	2003
Ellis Kinder (P)	1948–55
Walt Kinney (P)	1918
Bruce Kison (P)	1985
Billy Klaus (SS)	1955–58
Red Kleinow (C)	1910–11
Bob Kline (P)	1930–33
Ron Kline (P)	1969
Bob Klinger (P)	1946–47
Brent Knackert (P)	1996
John Knight (SS)	1907
Hal Kolstad (P)	1962–63
Cal Koonce (P)	1970–71
Andy Kosco (OF)	1972
Jack Kramer (P)	1948–49
Lew Krausse (P)	1972
Rick Kreuger (P)	1975–77
Rube Kroh (P)	1906–07
John Kroner (2B)	1935–36
Marty Krug (3B)	1912
Randy Kutcher (OF)	1988–90

L

Candy Lachance (1B)	1902–05
Kerry Lacy (P)	1996–97
Ty Laforest (3B)	1945
Roger Lafrancois (C)	1982
Joe Lahoud (OF)	1968–71
Eddie Lake (SS)	1943–45
Jack Lamabe (P)	1963–65
Bill Lamar (OF)	1919
Jeremy Lambert* (P)	2004
Dennis Lamp (P)	1988–91

Rick Lancellotti (1B)	1990	Steve Lomasney* (C)	1999
Bill Landis (P)	1967–69	George Lombard* (OF)	2005
Jim Landis (OF)	1967	Jim Lonborg (P)	1965–71
Sam Langford (OF)	1926	Walter Lonergan (2B)	1911
Carney Lansford (3B)	1981–82	Brian Looney (P)	1995
Mike Lansing (2B)	2000–01	Harry Lord (3B)	1907–10
Frank Laporte (2B)	1908	Derek Lowe* (P)	1997–04
John Larose (P)	1978	Johnny Lucas (OF)	1931–32
Lyn Lary (SS)	1934	Joe Lucey (P)	1925
Johnny Lazor (OF)	1943–46	Lou Lucier (P)	1943–44
Bill Lee (P)	1969–78	Del Lundgren (P)	1926–27
Dud Lee (SS)	1924–26	Tony Lupien (1B)	1940, 1942–43
Sang–Hoon Lee (P)	2000	Sparky Lyle (P)	1967–71
Bill Lefebvre (P)	1938–39	Walt Lynch (C)	1922
Lou Legett (C)	1933–35	Fred Lynn (OF)	1974–80
Regis Leheny (P)	1932	Brandon Lyon* (P)	2003
Paul Lehner (OF)	1952	Steve Lyons (OF)	1985–86, 1991–93
Nemo Leibold (OF)	1921–23		
John Leister (P)	1987, 1990	**M**	
Mark Lemke (2B)	1998	Danny MacFayden (P)	1926–32
Don Lenhardt (OF)	1952, 1954	Mike Macfarlane (C)	1995
Dutch Leonard (P)	1913–18	Alejandro Machado* (2B)	2005
Ted Lepcio (2B)	1952–59	Shane Mack (OF)	1997
Dutch Lerchen (SS)	1910	Billy Macleod (P)	1962
Louis Leroy (P)	1910	Keith Macwhorter (P)	1980
Curtis Leskanic (P)	2004	Bunny Madden (C)	1909–11
Darren Lewis (OF)	1998–01	Mike Maddux (P)	1995–96
Duffy Lewis (OF)	1910–17	Pete Magrini (P)	1966
Jack Lewis (2B)	1911	Ron Mahay* (P)	1995, 1997–98
Ted Lewis (P)	1901	Pat Mahomes* (P)	1996–97
Jim Leyritz (C)	1998	Chris Mahoney (P)	1910
John Lickert (C)	1981	Jim Mahoney (SS)	1959
Derek Lilliquist (P)	1995	Mark Malaska* (P)	2004
Johnny Lipon (SS)	1952–53	Jose Malave (OF)	1996–97
Hod Lisenbee (P)	1929–32	Jerry Mallett (OF)	1959
Dick Littlefield (P)	1950	Paul Maloy (P)	1913
Greg Litton (2B)	1994	Frank Malzone (3B)	1955–65
Don Lock (OF)	1969	Matt Mantei* (P)	2005
Skip Lockwood (P)	1980	Felix Mantilla (2B)	1963–65
George Loepp (OF)	1928	Jeff Manto (3B)	1996
James Lofton* (SS)	2001	Heinie Manush (OF)	1936
Tim Lollar (P)	1985–86	Josias Manzanillo* (P)	1991

Phil Marchildon (P)	1950	Archie McKain (P)	1937–38
Johnny Marcum (P)	1936–38	Walt McKeel (C)	1996–97
Juan Marichal (P)	1974	Jud McLaughlin (P)	1931–33
Ollie Marquardt (2B)	1931	Larry McLean (C)	1901
Bill Marshall (2B)	1931	Doc McMahon (P)	1908
Mike Marshall (OF)	1990–91	Don McMahon (P)	1966–67
Babe Martin (OF)	1948–49	Marty McManus (2B)	1931–33
Anastacio Martinez* (P)	2004	Norm McMillan (3B)	1923
Pedro Martinez* (P)	1998–99, 2002–04	Billy McMillon* (OF)	2005
Ramon Martinez (P)	2000	Eric McNair (SS)	1936–38
Sandy Martinez* (C)	2004	Mike McNally (2B)	1915–17, 1919–20
John Marzano (C)	1987–92	Gordon McNaughton (P)	1932
Walt Masterson (P)	1949–52	Jeff McNeely (OF)	1993
Tom Matchick (SS)	1970	Norm McNeil (C)	1919
William Matthews (P)	1909	Bill McWilliams (—)	1931
Gene Mauch (2B)	1956–57	Jesus Medrano* (2B)	2004
Charlie Maxwell (OF)	1950–52, 1954	Roman Mejias (OF)	1963–64
Wally Mayer (C)	1917–18	Sam Mele (OF)	1947–49, 1954–55
Chick Maynard (SS)	1922	Jose Melendez (P)	1993–94
Carl Mays (P)	1915–19	Ski Melillo (2B)	1935–37
Dick McAuliffe (2B)	1974–75	Bob Melvin (C)	1993
Tom McBride (OF)	1943–47	Ramiro Mendoza* (P)	2003
Dick McCabe (P)	1918	Mike Menosky (OF)	1920–23
Windy McCall (P)	1948–49	Mike Meola (P)	1933, 1936
Emmett McCann (SS)	1926	Orlando Merced* (OF)	1998
Tom McCarthy (P)	1985	Andy Merchant (C)	1975–76
David McCarty* (1B)	2003–05	Kent Mercker* (P)	1999
Tim McCarver (C)	1974–75	Cla Meredith* (P)	2005
Amby McConnell (2B)	1908–10	Spike Merena (P)	1934
Mickey McDermott (P)	1948–53	Lou Merloni* (2B)	1998–03
Allen McDill (P)	2001	Jack Merson (2B)	1953
Jim McDonald (P)	1950	Catfish Metkovich (OF)	1943–46
Ed McFarland (C)	1908	Russ Meyer (P)	1957
Eddie McGah (C)	1946–47	John Michaels (P)	1932
Willie McGee (OF)	1995	Dick Midkiff (P)	1938
Lynn McGlothen (P)	1972–73	Doug Mientkiewicz* (1B)	2004
Art McGovern (C)	1905	Dee Miles (OF)	1943
Bob McGraw (P)	1919	Kevin Millar* (1B)	2003–05
Deacon McGuire (C)	1907–08	Bing Miller (OF)	1935–36
Jim McHale (OF)	1908	Elmer Miller (OF)	1922
Marty McHale (P)	1910–11, 1916	Hack Miller (OF)	1918
Stuffy McInnis (1B)	1918–21	Otto Miller (3B)	1930–32

Rick Miller (OF)	1971–77, 1981–85	Frank Mulroney (P)	1930
Wade Miller* (P)	2005	Bill Mundy (1B)	1913
Dick Mills (P)	1970	Johnny Murphy (P)	1947
Buster Mills (OF)	1937	Rob Murphy (P)	1989–90
Rudy Minarcin (P)	1956–57	Tom Murphy (P)	1976–77
Nate Minchey (P)	1993–94, 1996	Walter Murphy (P)	1931
Doug Mirabelli* (C)	2001–05	George Murray (P)	1923–24
Charlie Mitchell (P)	1984–85	Matt Murray (P)	1995
Fred Mitchell (P)	1901–02	Tony Muser (1B)	1969
Johnny Mitchell (SS)	1922–23	Paul Musser (P)	1919
Keith Mitchell (OF)	1998	Alex Mustaikis (P)	1940
Kevin Mitchell (OF)	1996	Buddy Myer (2B)	1927–28
Herb Moford (P)	1959	Elmer Myers (P)	1920–22
Vince Molyneaux (P)	1918	Hap Myers (1B)	1910–11
Bill Monbouquette (P)	1958–65	Mike Myers* (P)	2005
Freddie Moncewicz (SS)	1928		
Bob Montgomery (C)	1970–79	**N**	
Bill Moore (C)	1926–27	Chris Nabholz (P)	1994
Wilcy Moore (P)	1931–32	Tim Naehring (3B)	1990–97
Andy Morales* (—)	2002	Judge Nagle (P)	1911
Dave Morehead (P)	1963–68	Mike Nagy (P)	1969–72
Roger Moret (P)	1970–75	Bill Narleski (SS)	1929–30
Cy Morgan (P)	1907–09	Blaine Neal* (P)	2005
Ed Morgan (1B)	1934	Ernie Neitzke (OF)	1921
Red Morgan (3B)	1906	Bryant Nelson* (2B)	2002
Ed Morris (P)	1928–31	Joe Nelson* (P)	2004
Frank Morrissey (P)	1901	Hal Neubauer (P)	1925
Guy Morton (—)	1954	Don Newhauser (P)	1972–74
Kevin Morton (P)	1991	Jeff Newman (C)	1983–84
Earl Moseley (P)	1913	Bobo Newsom (P)	1937
Walter Moser (P)	1911	Dick Newsome (P)	1941–43
Jerry Moses (C)	1965, 1968–70	Skeeter Newsome (SS)	1941–45
Wally Moses (OF)	1946–48	Gus Niarhos (C)	1952–53
Doc Moskiman (1B)	1910	Chet Nichols (P)	1960–63
Les Moss (C)	1951	Reid Nichols (OF)	1980–85
Jamie Moyer* (P)	1996	Al Niemiec (2B)	1934
Bill Mueller* (3B)	2003–05	Harry Niles (OF)	1908–10
Gordie Mueller (P)	1950	Al Nipper (P)	1983–87
Billy Muffett (P)	1960–62	Merlin Nippert (P)	1962
Greg Mulleavy (SS)	1933	Otis Nixon (OF)	1994
Freddie Muller (2B)	1933–34	Russ Nixon (C)	1960–65, 1968
Joe Mulligan (P)	1934	Trot Nixon* (RF)	1996, 1998–05

Willard Nixon (P)	1950–58
Hideo Nomo* (P)	2001
Red Nonnenkamp (OF)	1938–40
Chet Nourse (P)	1909
Les Nunamaker (C)	1911–14
Jon Nunnally* (OF)	1999

O

Mike O'Berry (C)	1979
Buck O'Brien (P)	1911–13
Jack O'Brien (OF)	1903
Syd O'Brien (3B)	1969
Tommy O'Brien (OF)	1949–50
Lefty O'Doul (OF)	1923
Mike O'Keefe* (1B)	2004
Troy O'Leary* (OF)	1995–01
Bill O'Neill (OF)	1904
Emmett O'Neill (P)	1943–45
Steve O'Neill (C)	1924
Frank O'Rourke (3B)	1922
Frank Oberlin (P)	1906–07
Jose Offerman* (1B)	1999–02
Ben Oglivie (OF)	1971–73
Tomo Ohka* (P)	2001
Bob Ojeda (P)	1980–85
Len Okrie (C)	1952
John Olerud* (1B)	2005
Darren Oliver* (P)	2002
Gene Oliver (C)	1968
Joe Oliver* (C)	2001
Tom Oliver (OF)	1930–33
Hank Olmsted (P)	1905
Karl Olson (OF)	1951, 1953–55
Marv Olson (2B)	1931–33
Ted Olson (P)	1936–38
Steve Ontiveros (P)	2000
George Orme (OF)	1920
David Ortiz* (DH)	2003–05
Luis Ortiz* (3B)	1993–94
Dan Osinski (P)	1966–67
Harry Ostdiek (C)	1908
Fritz Ostermueller (P)	1934–40

Johnny Ostrowski (OF)	1948
Marv Owen (3B)	1940
Mickey Owen (C)	1954
Spike Owen (SS)	1986–88
Frank Owens (C)	1905
Jeremy Owens* (CF)	2003–04

P

Jim Pagliaroni (C)	1955, 1960–62
Mike Palm (P)	1948
Jim Pankovits (2B)	1990
Al Papai (P)	1950
Larry Pape (P)	1909, 1911–12
Jonathan Papelbon* (P)	2005
Stan Papi (3B)	1979–80
Freddy Parent (SS)	1901–07
Mel Parnell (P)	1947–56
Larry Parrish (3B)	1988
Roy Partee (C)	1943–44, 1946–47
Stan Partenheimer (P)	1944
Ben Paschal (OF)	1920
Case Patten (P)	1908
Hank Patterson (C)	1932
Marty Pattin (P)	1972–73
Don Pavletich (C)	1970–71
Mike Paxton (P)	1977
Jay Payton* (OF)	2005
Johnny Peacock (C)	1937–44
Eddie Pellagrini (SS)	1946–47
Rudy Pemberton* (RF)	1996–97
Alejandro Pena (P)	1995
Jesus Pena* (P)	2000–01
Juan Pena* (P)	1999
Tony Pena (C)	1990–93
Brad Pennington (P)	1996
Herb Pennock (P)	1915–17, 1919–22, 1934
Juan Perez* (P)	2004
Tony Perez (1B)	1980–82
Matt Perisho* (P)	2005
John Perrin (OF)	1921
Robert Person* (P)	2003
Bill Pertica (P)	1918

Johnny Pesky (SS)	1942, 1946–52
Roberto Petagine* (1B)	2005
Gary Peters (P)	1970–72
Bob Peterson (C)	1906–07
Rico Petrocelli (SS)	1963, 1965–76
Dan Petry (P)	1991
Dave Philley (OF)	1962
Ed Phillips (P)	1970
Hipolito Pichardo (P)	2000–01
Val Picinich (C)	1923–25
Calvin Pickering* (DH)	2001
Urbane Pickering (3B)	1931–32
Jeff Pierce (P)	1995
Bill Piercy (P)	1922–24
Jim Piersall (OF)	1950, 1952–58
George Pipgras (P)	1933–35
Greg Pirkl (1B)	1996
Pinky Pittinger (SS)	1921–23
Juan Pizarro (P)	1968–69
Phil Plantier (OF)	1990–92
Herb Plews (2B)	1959
Jeff Plympton (P)	1991
Jennings Poindexter (P)	1936
Dick Pole (P)	1973–76
Nick Polly (3B)	1945
Ralph Pond (OF)	1910
Tom Poquette (OF)	1979, 1981
Dick Porter (OF)	1934
Bob Porterfield (P)	1956–58
Mark Portugal (P)	1999
Nels Potter (P)	1941
Ken Poulsen (3B)	1967
Arquimedez Pozo (3B)	1996–97
Larry Pratt (C)	1914
Del Pratt (2B)	1921–22
George Prentiss (P)	1901–02
Joe Price (P)	1989
Curtis Pride* (OF)	1997, 2000
Doc Prothro (3B)	1925
Tex Pruiett (P)	1907–08
Bill Pulsipher* (P)	2001
Billy Purtell (3B)	1910–11

Frankie Pytlak (C)	1941, 1945–46
Q	
Paul Quantrill* (P)	1992–94
Jack Quinn (P)	1922–25
Frank Quinn (P)	1949–50
Rey Quinones (SS)	1986
Carlos Quintana (1B)	1988–91, 1993
R	
Dick Radatz (P)	1962–66
Dave Rader (C)	1980
Chuck Rainey (P)	1979–82
Hanley Ramirez* (SS)	2005
Manny Ramirez* (OF)	2001–05
Pat Rapp (P)	1999
Jeff Reardon (P)	1990–92
Johnny Reder (1B)	1932
Jerry Reed (P)	1990
Jody Reed (2B)	1987–92
Pokey Reese* (2B)	2004
Bobby Reeves (3B)	1929–31
Bill Regan (2B)	1926–30
Wally Rehg (OF)	1913–15
Dick Reichle (OF)	1922–23
Mike Remlinger* (P)	2005
Win Remmerswaal (P)	1979–80
Jerry Remy (2B)	1978–84
Steve Renko (P)	1979–80
Bill Renna (OF)	1958–59
Edgar Renteria* (SS)	2005
Rip Repulski (OF)	1960–61
Carlos Reyes (P)	1998
Carl Reynolds (OF)	1934–35
Gordon Rhodes (P)	1932–35
Karl Rhodes (OF)	1995
Hal Rhyne (SS)	1929–32
Jim Rice (OF)	1974–89
Woody Rich (P)	1939–41
Jeff Richardson (SS)	1993
Al Richter (SS)	1951, 1953
Paul Rigdon* (P)	2004

Joe Riggert (OF)	1911	Allan Russell (P)	1919–22
Topper Rigney (SS)	1926–27	Jack Russell (P)	1926–32, 1936
Ernest Riles (SS)	1993	Jeff Russell (P)	1993–94
Allen Ripley (P)	1978–79	Rip Russell (1B)	1946–47
Walt Ripley (P)	1935	Babe Ruth (OF)	1914–19
Pop Rising (OF)	1905	Jack Ryan (P)	1909
Jay Ritchie (P)	1964–65	Jack Ryan (OF)	1929
Luis Rivera (SS)	1989–93	Ken Ryan (P)	1992–95
Dave Roberts* (CF)	2004	Mike Ryan (C)	1964–67
Billy Jo Robidoux (1B)	1990	Mike Ryba (P)	1941–46
Aaron Robinson (C)	1951	Gene Rye (OF)	1931
Floyd Robinson (OF)	1968		
Jack Robinson (P)	1949	**S**	
Mike Rochford (P)	1988–90	Bret Saberhagen (P)	1997–99
Bill Rodgers (2B)	1915	Donnie Sadler* (OF)	1998–00
Carlos Rodriguez (SS)	1994–95	Bob Sadowski (P)	1966
Frankie Rodriguez* (P)	1995	Ed Sadowski (C)	1960
Steve Rodriguez (2B)	1995	Joe Sambito (P)	1986–87
Tony Rodriguez (SS)	1996	Anibal Sanchez* (P)	2005
Billy Rogell (SS)	1925, 1927–28	Freddy Sanchez* (3B)	2002–03
Lee Rogers (P)	1938	Rey Sanchez* (SS)	2002
Garry Roggenburk (P)	1966, 1968–69	Ken Sanders (P)	1966
Billy Rohr (P)	1967	Marino Santana (P)	1999
Red Rollings (3B)	1927–28	Jose Santiago (P)	1966–70
Ed Romero (SS)	1986–89	Angel Santos* (2B)	2001
Mandy Romero* (C)	1998	Tom Satriano (C)	1969–70
Kevin Romine (OF)	1985–91	Scott Sauerbeck* (P)	2003
Vicente Romo (P)	1969–70	Dave Sax (C)	1985–87
Brett Roneberg* (RF)	2004	Bill Sayles (P)	1939
Buddy Rosar (C)	1950–51	Ray Scarborough (P)	1951–52
Brian Rose* (P)	1997–00	Russ Scarritt (OF)	1929–31
Si Rosenthal (OF)	1925–26	Wally Schang (C)	1918–20
Buster Ross (P)	1924–26	Charley Schanz (P)	1950
Braggo Roth (OF)	1919	Bob Scherbarth (C)	1950
Jack Rothrock (OF)	1925–32	Chuck Schilling (2B)	1961–65
Rich Rowland (C)	1994–95	Curt Schilling* (P)	2004
Stan Royer (3B)	1994	Calvin Schiraldi (P)	1986–87
Joe Rudi (OF)	1981	Rudy Schlesinger (—)	1965
Muddy Ruel (C)	1921–22, 1931	Biff Schlitzer (P)	1909
Red Ruffing (P)	1924–30	George Schmees (OF)	1952
Pete Runnels (1B)	1958–62	Dave Schmidt (C)	1981
Ryan Rupe* (P)	2003	Johnny Schmitz (P)	1956

Dick Schofield (SS)	1969–70	Norm Siebern (1B)	1967–68
Pete Schourek (P)	1998, 2000–01	Sonny Siebert (P)	1969–73
Tony Schrager* (SS)	2005	Al Simmons (OF)	1943
Ossee Schreckengost (C)	1901	Pat Simmons (P)	1928–29
Al Schroll (P)	1958–59	Dave Sisler (P)	1956–59
Don Schwall (P)	1961–62	Ted Sizemore (2B)	1979–80
Everett Scott (SS)	1914–21	Camp Skinner (OF)	1923
George Scott (1B)	1966–71, 1977–79	Craig Skok (P)	1973
Rudy Seanez* (P)	2003	Jack Slattery (C)	1901
Tom Seaver (P)	1986	Steve Slayton (P)	1928
Bob Seeds (OF)	1933–34	Heathcliff Slocumb (P)	1996–97
Diego Segui (P)	1974–75	Charlie Small (OF)	1930
Phil Seibel* (P)	2004	Al Smith (OF)	1964
Kip Selbach (OF)	1904–06	Aleck Smith (C)	1903
Bill Selby* (3B)	1996	Bob Smith (P)	1955
Aaron Sele* (P)	1993–97	Bob Smith (P)	1958
Jeff Sellers (P)	1985–88	Charlie Smith (P)	1909–11
Brian Sellier* (OF)	2004	Chris Smith* (P)	2005
Merle Settlemire (P)	1928	Dan Smith* (P)	2000
Wally Shaner (OF)	1926–27	Doug Smith (P)	1912
Howie Shanks (OF)	1923–24	Eddie Smith (P)	1947
Red Shannon (2B)	1919	Elmer Smith (OF)	1922
Jon Shave* (SS)	2000–01	Frank Smith (P)	1910–11
Al Shaw (C)	1907	George Smith (P)	1930
John Shea (P)	1928	George Smith (2B)	1966
Merv Shea (C)	1933	John Smith (1B)	1931
Danny Sheaffer (C)	1987	Lee Smith (P)	1988–90
Dave Shean (2B)	1918–19	Paddy Smith (C)	1920
Andy Sheets* (SS)	2000	Pete Smith (P)	1962–63
Rollie Sheldon (P)	1966	Reggie Smith (OF)	1966–73
Keith Shepherd (P)	1995	Zane Smith (P)	1995
Neill Sheridan (—)	1948	Mike Smithson (P)	1988–89
Ben Shields (P)	1930	Wally Snell (C)	1913
Jason Shiell* (P)	2003	Chris Snopek (3B)	1998
Strick Shofner (3B)	1947	Earl Snyder* (1B)	2004
Kelly Shoppach* (C)	2005	Moose Solters (OF)	1934–35
Ernie Shore (P)	1914–17	Rudy Sommers (P)	1926–27
Bill Short (P)	1966	Allen Sothoron (P)	1921
Chick Shorten (OF)	1915–17	Bill Spanswick (P)	1964
Brian Shouse* (P)	1998	Tully Sparks (P)	1902
Terry Shumpert* (2B)	1995	Tris Speaker (OF)	1907–15
Joe Siddall (C)	2000	Stan Spence (OF)	1940–41, 1948–49

Tubby Spencer (C)	1909	Denny Sullivan (OF)	1907–08
Andy Spognardi (2B)	1932	Frank Sullivan (P)	1953–60
Ed Sprague (3B)	2000	Haywood Sullivan (C)	1955, 1957, 1959–60
Jack Spring (P)	1957	Marc Sullivan (C)	1982, 1984–87
Bobby Sprowl (P)	1978	Carl Sumner (OF)	1928
Chick Stahl (OF)	1901–06	Jeff Suppan* (P)	1995–97, 2003
Jake Stahl (1B)	1903, 1908–10, 1912–13	George Susce (P)	1955–58
Matt Stairs* (OF)	1995	Bill Swanson (2B)	1914
Tracy Stallard (P)	1960–62	Bill Sweeney (1B)	1930–31
Jerry Standaert (2B)	1929	Greg Swindell* (P)	1998
Lee Stange (P)	1966–70	Len Swormstedt (P)	1906
Rob Stanifer* (P)	2000		
Bob Stanley (P)	1977–89	**T**	
Mike Stanley (C)	1996–00	Jim Tabor (3B)	1938–44
Jack Stansbury (3B)	1918	Doug Taitt (OF)	1928–29
Mike Stanton* (P)	1995–96	Frank Tanana (P)	1981
Dave Stapleton (1B)	1980–86	Jesse Tannehill (P)	1904–08
Jigger Statz (OF)	1920	Arlie Tarbert (OF)	1927–28
Elmer Steele (P)	1907–09	Jose Tartabull (OF)	1966–68
Ben Steiner (2B)	1945–46	La Schelle Tarver (OF)	1986
Red Steiner (C)	1945	Willie Tasby (OF)	1960
Mike Stenhouse (OF)	1986	Bennie Tate (C)	1932
Gene Stephens (OF)	1952–53, 1955–60	Jim Tatum (1B)	1996
Vern Stephens (SS)	1948–52	Ken Tatum (P)	1971–73
Jerry Stephenson (P)	1963, 1965–68	Jesus Tavarez (OF)	1997
Adam Stern* (OF)	2005	Harry Taylor (P)	1950–52
Sammy Stewart (P)	1986	Scott Taylor (P)	1992–93
Dick Stigman (P)	1966	Birdie Tebbetts (C)	1947–50
Carl Stimson (P)	1923	Yank Terry (P)	1940, 1942–45
Chuck Stobbs (P)	1947–51	Jake Thielman (P)	1908
Al Stokes (C)	1925–26	Blaine Thomas (P)	1911
Dean Stone (P)	1957	Brad Thomas* (P)	2004
George Stone (OF)	1903	Fred Thomas (3B)	1918
Jeff Stone (OF)	1989–90	George Thomas (OF)	1966–71
Howie Storie (C)	1931–32	Lee Thomas (OF)	1964–65
Lou Stringer (2B)	1948–50	Pinch Thomas (C)	1912–17
Amos Strunk (OF)	1918–19	Tommy Thomas (P)	1937
Dick Stuart (1B)	1963–64	Bobby Thomson (OF)	1960
George Stumpf (OF)	1931–33	Jack Thoney (OF)	1908–09, 1911
Tom Sturdivant (P)	1960	Hank Thormahlen (P)	1921
Chris Stynes* (3B)	2001	Faye Throneberry (OF)	1952, 1955–57
Jim Suchecki (P)	1950	Luis Tiant (P)	1971–78

Bob Tillman (C)	1962–67
Mike Timlin* (P)	2003–05
Lee Tinsley (OF)	1994–96
Jack Tobin (OF)	1926–27
Johnny Tobin (3B)	1945
Phil Todt (1B)	1924–30
Kevin Tolar* (P)	2002–03
Andy Tomberlin (OF)	1994
Denney Tomori* (P)	2005
Tony Tonneman (C)	1911
Mike Torrez (P)	1978–82
John Trautwein (P)	1988
Joe Trimble (P)	1955
Ricky Trlicek (P)	1994, 1997
Dizzy Trout (P)	1952
Frank Truesdale (2B)	1918
Mike Trujillo (P)	1985–86
John Tudor (P)	1979–83
Bob Turley (P)	1963

U

Tom Umphlett (OF)	1953
Bob Unglaub (1B)	1904–05, 1907–08
Ugueth Urbina* (P)	2002

V

Tex Vache (OF)	1925
Pedro Valdes (LF)	1999–00
Carlos Valdez (P)	1998
Julio Valdez (SS)	1980–83
Sergio Valdez (P)	1994
John Valentin (SS)	1992–01
Dave Valle (C)	1994
Ben Van Dyke (P)	1912
Tim Van Egmond (P)	1994–95
Al Vancamp (OF)	1931–32
Hy Vandenberg (P)	1935
Jason Varitek* (C)	1997–05
Mo Vaughn (1B)	1991–98
Ramon Vazquez* (SS)	2005
Bobby Veach (OF)	1924–25

Bob Veale (P)	1972–74
Dario Veras (P)	1998
Wilton Veras (3B)	1999–00
Mickey Vernon (1B)	1956–57
Sammy Vick (OF)	1921
Frank Viola (P)	1992–94
Ossie Vitt (3B)	1919–21
Clyde Vollmer (OF)	1950–53
Jake Volz (P)	1901
Joe Vosmik (OF)	1938–39

W

Jake Wade (P)	1939
Charlie Wagner (P)	1938–42, 1946
Gary Wagner (P)	1969–70
Hal Wagner (C)	1944, 1946–47
Heinie Wagner (SS)	1906–13, 1915, 1916, 1918
Tim Wakefield* (P)	1995–05
Rube Walberg (P)	1934–37
Chico Walker (OF)	1980–81, 1983–84
Tilly Walker (OF)	1916–17
Todd Walker* (2B)	2003
Murray Wall (P)	1957–59
Jimmy Walsh (OF)	1916–17
Bucky Walters (P)	1933–34
Fred Walters (C)	1945
Roxy Walters (C)	1919–23
Bill Wambsganss (2B)	1924–25
Pee-Wee Wanninger (SS)	1927
John Warner (C)	1902
Rabbit Warstler (SS)	1930–33
John Wasdin* (P)	1997–00
Gary Waslewski (P)	1967–68
Bob Watson (1B)	1979
Johnny Watwood (OF)	1932–33
Monte Weaver (P)	1939
Earl Webb (OF)	1930–32
Lenny Webster (C)	1999
Ray Webster (2B)	1960
Eric Wedge (DH)	1991–92, 1994
Bob Weiland (P)	1932–34

Frank Welch (OF)	1927	George Winn (P)	1919
Herb Welch (SS)	1925	Herm Winningham (OF)	1992
Johnny Welch (P)	1932–36	Tom Winsett (OF)	1930–31, 1933
David Wells* (P)	2005	George Winter (P)	1901–08
Tony Welzer (P)	1926–27	Clarence Winters (P)	1924
Fred Wenz (P)	1968–69	Rick Wise (P)	1974–77
Billy Werber (3B)	1933–36	Johnnie Wittig (P)	1949
Bill Werle (P)	1953–54	Bob Wolcott (P)	1998–99
Vic Wertz (OF)	1959–61	Larry Wolfe (3B)	1979–80
David West (P)	1998	Harry Wolter (OF)	1909
Matt White* (P)	2003	Joe Wood (OF)	1908–15
Sammy White (C)	1951–59	Joe Wood (P)	1944
George Whiteman (OF)	1907, 1918	Ken Wood (OF)	1952
Mark Whiten (OF)	1995	Wilbur Wood (P)	1961–64
Ernie Whitt (C)	1976	Steve Woodard* (P)	2003
Al Widmar (P)	1947	John Woods (P)	1924
Bill Wight (P)	1951–52	Pinky Woods (P)	1943–45
Del Wilber (C)	1952–54	Bob Woodward (P)	1985–88
Joe Wilhoit (OF)	1919	Shawn Wooten* (C)	2005
Dana Williams (DH)	1989	Hoge Workman (P)	1924
Dave Williams (P)	1902	Al Worthington (P)	1960
Denny Williams (OF)	1924–25, 1928	Jim Wright (P)	1978–79
Dib Williams (2B)	1935	Tom Wright (OF)	1948–51
Dick Williams (OF)	1963–64	John Wyatt (P)	1966–68
Ken Williams (OF)	1928–29	Weldon Wyckoff (P)	1916–18
Rip Williams (C)	1911		
Stan Williams (P)	1972	**Y**	
Ted Williams (OF)	1939–42, 1946–60	Carl Yastrzemski (OF)	1961–83
Scott Williamson* (P)	2004	Steve Yerkes (2B)	1909, 1911–14
Jim Willoughby (P)	1975–77	Rudy York (1B)	1946–47
Ted Wills (P)	1959–62	Kevin Youkilis* (3B)	2004–05
Archie Wilson (OF)	1952	Cy Young (P)	1901–08
Duane Wilson (P)	1958	Matt Young (P)	1991–92
Earl Wilson (P)	1959–60, 1962–66	Tim Young* (P)	2000
Gary Wilson (2B)	1902		
Jack Wilson (P)	1935–41	**Z**	
Jim Wilson (P)	1945–46	Paul Zahniser (P)	1925–26
John Wilson (P)	1927–28	Al Zarilla (OF)	1949–50, 1952–53
Les Wilson (OF)	1911	Norm Zauchin (1B)	1951, 1955–57
Squanto Wilson (C)	1914	Matt Zeiser (P)	1914
Hal Wiltse (P)	1926–28	Bill Zuber (P)	1946–47
Ted Wingfield (P)	1924–27	Bob Zupcic (OF)	1991–94